HOW TO STOP BEING A
NARCISSIST

Overcome the Toxic Narcissism that is
Sabotaging Your Relationships

LUCAS BAILEY

Your FREE Bonuses

Download the following 2 bonuses for free as supplements to the main book.

Bonus 1:

Bonus 2:

- Rid Yourself of the beliefs that limit your life.
- Includes both online and offline strategies.
- What effort gives the best rewards.
  And more...

To Download Your 2 Free Bonuses:

5 Toxic Beliefs and Their Cures

13 Strategies for Making Friends Outside of Work

Scan the QR code below with the camara function on your cell phone and click the link.

"And we need to know what it is to be human if we are to avoid becoming narcissists."

- ALEXANDER LOWEN

Download the Audio Version of this Book for FREE

If you love listening to audiobooks on-the-go or would enjoy a narration as you read along, I have a great news for you. You can download the full audiobook version of *How to Stop Being a Narcissist* for FREE (Regularly $14.95) just by signing up for a FREE 30-day Audible trial with one of the links below!

Scan a QR Code Below to Get Started:

Audiobook US   Audiobook UK

Contents

HOW TO STOP BEING A
NARCISSIST

INTRODUCTION

If you are the target audience, by picking up this book, you have proven that you are well on your way to self-improvement. Chances are you are a narcissist or at least have some narcissistic tendencies and, more importantly, you are starting to get sick of them. Maybe someone had a heart-to-heart with you about how you don't care, don't listen, and how they feel like more of a tool than an actual person. Maybe you have come to realize you don't have as many friends as you thought, or perhaps you find living your life as a slave to the approval of others is just exhausting. Regardless of the source, this desire for change is commendable.

You might be feeling conflicted. The world has told you repeatedly that you cannot change, that you are a monster, and are deserving of swift disproportionate consequences. Everyone should point and laugh at you while you lay in the mud. The bottom line is that you might feel utterly alone in this, which is not entirely wrong.

Before we start, we should review what this book is and is not. This is meant for a person who is a narcissist or that has narcissistic traits and wants to improve. This is not a book on outsmarting or detecting a narcissist. This book is written with the understanding that anyone is capable of real human growth. While we will examine narcissists whose actions have caused harm to themselves and others, it is not coming from the angle that narcissists are evil or conniving people that need to be put in their place or receive retribution. Many of these behaviors are rooted in mental health and coping with a traumatic world. Think of narcissism as more of a fuel than a spark.

However, this book is not going to coddle you either. Whether you want to admit it or are even capable of seeing it at all, your actions and thought patterns, regardless of their source, have probably hurt you and someone else. To begin the healing process, you must come to terms with the effects of your actions. Your first lesson is that how you perceive or intend something does not matter when someone else is demonstrably hurt. You will learn how narcissistic actions look from the outside, what they may look like from the inner recesses of your mind, and how to begin the process of unlearning. It will feel like peeling off a suit of armor you have been wearing your entire life, piece by piece. You may realize that armor was more like taking a security blanket to war.

Your real armor, sword, and shield will be learning what it is to be a good person, how to empathize, and what that means to others instead of just you.

Here is the rub, though, philosophers have grappled with that question since Plato, and we will also examine that fact. It's easy to think that people are born good or bad because that frees society up of any responsibility of teaching people to be one way or the other. The truth is that goodness is predicated on a social contract instead of purely on DNA. A person that has faced life never knowing love, proper social interaction, or learning basic morality has very little chance of becoming what society deems as good. Some people point to sociopaths and serial killers that showed red flags from the start despite growing up in a typical household, but these are exceptions and not the rule. The fact that therapy and medications can be wildly successful, especially at most early interventions, proves that your destiny was never set in stone.

Mental health is not your fault, but it is your responsibility.

- Marcus Parks, Last Podcast on The Left

WHAT IS NARCISSISM?

"If someone corrects you, and you feel offended, then YOU have an EGO problem."

- NOUMAN ALI KHAN

Narcissistic Personality Disorder (or NPD) is a personality disorder characterized by incredibly self-centered thoughts and behaviors. A need for attention or being seen as special or important is prevalent. NPD is part of the Cluster B personality disorders that include bipolar, antisocial, borderline, and histrionic personality disorders. Their unifying traits are unpredictable behaviors, inability to regulate emotions, and overall dramatic nature.

Doctors know that narcissism can manifest in different ways, so they have developed a diagnosis system to take that into account. They have curated a list of behaviors and personality traits associated with narcissism; a person must meet five to be diagnosed (Mayo Clinic, n.d.).

1. An inflated sense of self-importance to the point that they exaggerate achievements.

2. Delusions of grandeur.

3. The belief that you are special and cannot be seen associating with or be understood by the peasants.

4. A pervasive need for acknowledgment and adoration.

5. Having an entitled need for special treatment.

6. Taking advantage of others for personal gain.

7. Is easily consumed by envy but also believes that everyone is envious of them.

8. Transparently arrogant behaviors and beliefs.

The Nature of Narcissism

Before we understand the social causes of narcissism, one must understand the biological causes. It should be noted that studies on narcissists can be a bit sparse compared to other disorders. To study something, a volunteer needs to recognize they have the condition and sign up to take surveys, talk about their feelings, and get shoved in an MRI machine. This is a tall order for anyone; let alone a narcissist who is not conscious of their behavior. However, scientists have been making progress in their research. For one, the disorder can run in families (Torgersen et al., 2012), so people born to narcissistic parents deal with a predisposition and the psychological elements in a two-fold assault. However, which traits you get are more up in the air. A grandiose narcissist will not necessarily create a mini-me based on genetics alone. They can end up with a vulnerable narcissist, or their kid can beat the odds (Luo et al., 2014).

Unfortunately, growing up in a narcissistic household can irreparably affect the development of a child's brain, namely in the hippocampus and the amygdala. If you have been paying attention to neuroscience, you would know that those regions are important to learning, memories, and emotional regulation (*The Neuroscience of Narcissism and Narcissistic Abuse | CPTSDfoundation.Org*, 2020). As such, you have a child that can have trouble in school and can't quite remember what they were told. This can lead to intense frustration in any child, and without the proper means to control their temper, they quickly become "problem children" in school. This further shatters their self-esteem as school is a child's whole life. They may miss certain milestones and internalize this identity as a poor student. They have nowhere that they can feel love, accomplishment, and pride. They may seek out these emotions from other sources but can never cultivate that energy independently because they never had a chance.

Another brain region abnormality that is commonly found in narcissists resides in the anterior cingulate cortex. This part of the brain is responsible for certain cognitive functions, such as empathy. There is the dorsal anterior cingulate cortex (dACC) which can have an effect on attachment style and someone's reaction to rejection. A person with an avoidant attachment style will most likely have a decrease in activity in this area while someone with an anxious attachment style has higher activity in this area (Cascio et al., 2015). This comes into play because increased activity here will make someone incredibly sensitive to any perceived rejection, potentially to the point of aggression (Chester & DeWall, 2016).

Finally, there is the anterior insula which is not only associated with empathy but also with salience or determining what is important. The default mode of this area is to be focused on the self. It makes sense; if humans don't take care of their needs first, they will die out and fail to help others effectively. However, narcissists never seem to develop the ability to turn this salience outward. As a result, they end up with a rigid sense of self-importance (Ekua Hagan, 2018).

The Health of a Narcissist

NPD does more than wreck your relationships; it can actually physically harm your heart. Living on the edge turns out to be bad for you! Since narcissists are always anticipating a negative outcome or displeasure, their heart rates are often elevated, which can contribute to heart disease later in life (Kelsey et al., 2001). It doesn't even need to be work or project related. The fear of rejection can make your heart spin out of control whenever you are confronted with a stressful social situation (Sommer et al., 2009).

People with NPD also tend to have higher cortisol levels (Edelstein et al., 2010). This means that you are so chronically stressed that your hormones are completely out of whack. Cortisol is like adrenaline light for a stressed-out body. It is stimulating but tends to have a delayed timer, so our bodies don't immediately crash once the adrenaline wears off. It's not meant to pump constantly, but it does because of chronic stress. This affects weight, skin, mood, and sleep; basically, everything we need to function. Getting a handle on your narcissism should be considered an act of self-care for the sake of your physical health.

Comorbidities of NPD

Eating Disorders

The same mental environment that allows NPD to take root is also incredibly fertile for eating disorders such as anorexia and bulimia (Sivanathan et al., 2019). Individuals with narcissistic traits tend to stake much of their identity on their self-image and physical appearance, coupled with a need for external validation and admiration. This preoccupation with the aesthetic can contribute to body dissatisfaction and body dysmorphia, which are core features of eating disorders. Both narcissism and eating disorders involve an obsession with control. Narcissists will control their bodies and food intake to maintain a desired image or assert dominance over themselves and their vices. This can manifest as restrictive eating patterns, binging and purging, or excessive exercise. Finally, underlying psychological factors such as low self-esteem, perfectionism, and emotional dysregulation can contribute heavily to narcissism and eating disorders. Eating disorders, especially anorexia, are one of the most self-destructive behaviors. Anorexia has the highest mortality rate of any mental illness, including those that make a person knowingly attempt suicide. While this level of self-destructive behavior seems antithetical to NPD, it actually tracks. The desire to be so accepted that one would deprive themselves of food to the point of wasting away has nothing to do with how much you think you love yourself. This exemplifies one of the most significant sticking points of narcissism; often, the first one hurt by it is you and you alone (Sivanathan et al., 2019).

Borderline Personality Disorder

The comorbidity between NPD and Borderline Personality Disorder (BPD) is well-documented thanks to their symptoms looking like a significantly overlapped Venn diagram. They have a ton in common, such as difficulties with self-identity and emotional regulation.

This can lead to challenges in diagnosis which can affect treatment and therapy. However, there is a third choice of comorbid NPD and BPD. These individuals may exhibit challenging behaviors, including unstable self-esteem, intense fear of abandonment, mood swings, and impulsive and self-destructive behaviors. This can make for a complex clinical picture, with individuals struggling to maintain stable relationships, cope with emotional distress, and establish a sense of self.

Treatment for comorbid NPD and BPD typically involves a combination of psychotherapy, focusing on building self-awareness and emotion regulation skills, and exploring underlying traumas or attachment issues. It requires a comprehensive and integrative approach that addresses the unique challenges of both disorders. It aims to foster healthier thought patterns that lead to a stable sense of self, healthier relationships, and emotional regulation. Needless to say, that this requires an experienced professional to tackle and openness to treatment (Hörz-Sagstetter et al., 2018).

Anxiety and Depression

People with NPD can experience comorbid depression and anxiety, which further feeds into their mental health issues. Just because it is characterized by grandiosity, self-centeredness, and a lack of empathy doesn't mean that the presence of depression and anxiety will add another layer of emotional distress. These individuals may struggle with feelings of worthlessness, emptiness, and persistent sadness, which can crush their self-esteem despite their outward evidence to the contrary. Additionally, anxiety may arise from a fear of failure, criticism, or not living up to perceived high standards. Narcissists can experience excessive worry, restlessness, and a fear of the unknown. This level of mental distress makes narcissists incredibly vulnerable to suicidality (Coleman et al., 2017). Never tell someone that a narcissist loves themselves too much even to consider that option. If you have ever dealt with these feelings, seek help immediately.

Addiction

Narcissists are particularly vulnerable to addictions, from chemical to behavioral. This feeling of invincibility coupled with either a need to prove yourself or fill a hole in your soul can drive anyone to addictive behaviors. Addiction is like the junk food version of human satisfaction. A scratch off ticket or a bottle of booze will eventually be the only way a narcissist at their lowest point can possibly escape their reality. They might be addicted to the fantasy that gambling provides or the fact that drinking lets them forget how dissatisfied with their lives they truly are (Jauk & Dieterich, 2019).

The History of Narcissism

Pride is considered the first sin. Before Adam and Eve, Lucifer was banished from heaven when he thought he could do a better job than God, and it was all downhill from there as a species. Many lessons in the Bible boil down to "humble yourself before God, or you will be subdued by a flood or be cursed with language diversity." The etymology of the word narcissism comes from the Ancient Greek story of Narcissus. In another parable meant to teach children the importance of humility, Narcissus was born an incredibly handsome hunter. He rejected all romantic advances in favor of his own reflection in a pool of water. Some stories have him melting away, and others have him committing suicide when he realizes his affection can never be reciprocated. He is now associated with a flower and a personality disorder, which would probably be a further blow to his pride.

The concept was not fully conceptualized until the 1900s. Before that, narcissism was seen more as a state of sexual perversion, a normal developmental stage, or looped in with psychopathy. It really started to take a familiar shape when Sigmund Freud came on the scene. He saw narcissism as part of a person's normal development, a form of love that starts inward and will eventually work out as a person matures and is exposed to more people that challenge their initial ego. To Freud, babies and children were narcissists because their immaturity made them incapable of empathy. He described this self-love as "ego-libido". When we grow and expand our horizons to other people and objects (there is a reason Freud has lost favor in the scientific community), that becomes "object-libido". If this object-libido redirects back inward, then Freud posited that while this can be a part of human development, it can also pathologize into something unmanageable later in life. According to Freud, the only antidote to this is caring for someone else, since that energy transfer leaves you with less ego to fester into narcissism (Zauraiz Lone, 2019).

Heinz Kohut expanded on Freud's theories, agreeing that narcissism is an infant's default predisposition that should eventually become healthy self-esteem, if all goes well. However, he introduced the idea that if a child is traumatized or neglected, narcissism enters into a state of arrested development, leading to the issues we see in some adults. He was also more charitable to the concept, stating that in certain circumstances, narcissism is just a form of resilience and self-assurance, which is a good thing at the end of the day (McLean, 2007).

Flavors of Narcissism

Overt/Grandiose Narcissist

Some narcissists are easier to spot than others. Your overt narcissist sticks out and is proud of it. That inner voice that projects doubt is tied up in the closet somewhere, and all it is left is pure, unadulterated confidence. Overts are boisterous, charming, and incredibly self-assured. These are your Gastons from *Beauty and the Beast*, Gilderoy Lockharts from *Harry Potter*, Walter Whites from *Breaking Bad*, and Jay Gatsbys. This narcissist needs to be the center of attention to help them achieve their career goals or ask someone on a date. However, if they don't have anything to back up all that hot air, they can quickly come off as grating and overwhelming to be around.

Antagonistic Narcissist

This type of narcissist is confident and thrives in conflict and looking for a fight. They hold grudges, are quick to anger, are consumed with winning, and cannot handle not having the upper hand. Examples include Alexander the Great (he literally thought he was the son of the god Zeus), Vegeta from *Dragon Ball Z*, and many elite athletes.

Covert/Vulnerable Narcissist

A fragility in their identity rules the covert narcissist who can have an introverted nature. They can still have whirlwind fantasies about how special they are, but they tend to keep it to themselves or don't actually believe it. Their main difference from overt narcissists is that they are incapable of self-assurance. Instead of screaming how they are the bee's knees from the rooftops, they tend to go through roundabout ways to get that admiration and attention and elevate their status. This can look like:

- Compliment fishing
- Passive aggressive comments
- Guilt-tripping
- Being performative in performing good deeds
- The non-apology apology

Examples of covert narcissists include Kendall Roy from *Succession*, Cersei Lannister from *Game of Thrones*, and Elanor Shellstrop from *The Good Place*.

Community Narcissist

These narcissists thrive in a crowd because they feel like they are better than everyone. These are the types who record themselves giving homeless people money because they have a warped sense of morality and justice. It is easy to justify bad behavior and haughty attitudes because they believe they are a net positive on the world.

Malignant Narcissist

This is controversial because there is no medical consensus on what constitutes malignant narcissism. Assuming they are a thing, think of it as narcissism in its final form. They are confident, self-centered, unempathetic, and crave power, but also relish in the pain of others, are violent, and are massively impulsive. Examples could include most dictators (probably El Chapo), and serial killers, such as Jeffery Dahmer and Jim Jones. In fiction, think of Frieza from *Dragon Ball Z*, Fire Lord Ozai from *Avatar the Last Airbender*, Michael from *The Good Place*, and Logan Roy from *Succession*.

What NPD is NOT

Everyone and their mother seem like narcissists in our selfie-obsessed culture. However, the word narcissist has become a bit of a buzzword for people we don't like. Every dubious pop psychology blog or YouTube channel has videos on why a particular celebrity must be a narcissist. The fact is that NPD has a precise medical definition. A professional must diagnose it, not someone who took psych 101 and now thinks they can weaponize it.

For one, there is NPD and narcissistic traits. Everyone can exhibit narcissistic characteristics from time to time. We lost our cool at an airport or a bank and were harsher than we were meant to be to an employee. When someone sits in traffic and fumes at everyone who also decided to take that same road - that can be considered narcissism. If these are passing behaviors, then that person is not a narcissist; they are just having a human reaction to being frustrated.

Being formally diagnosed with a psychological disorder has to impact your life or someone else's life negatively. There lies a spectrum of narcissistic traits, but you are probably just somewhere on that spectrum until you consistently show at least five of the above behaviors and at a cost.

People tend to conflate other disorders and behaviors with narcissism. These include:

- Not feeling love
- Lacking emotion
- Forgetting important dates
- Having confidence
- Having low emotional intelligence
- Having a sense of self-preservation

While these traits can exist in and be a part of NPD, they don't mean anything in a vacuum. Narcissism has become a cheap way to discredit someone. While the negative actions and lack of accountability a narcissist is capable of can be examined by society, just having the disorder should not be an immediate scarlet letter.

Upon our birth, we are all given a toolbox to navigate life. That box is messed with repeatedly as we age. A well-adjusted neurotypical person has everything they need to interact with others and deal with anything life throws at them. They have one of those excellent multi-tiered toolboxes that you see at a mechanics shop with everything you need to build a house and fix a Ferrari.

Someone that is neurodivergent has no such luxury. In the case of a narcissist, their self-awareness-hammer might be rusted, and their empathy-drill might be missing half of the bits; someone borrowed their ability-to-accept-criticism-screwdriver and never returned it, and the ego that acts as the box is cracked and faded.

This is not something anybody chooses. Multiple factors, such as genetics, brain structure, and mental health, come into play, but the web is so complex it's hard to determine the source. Still, most research finds that narcissists are made that way during their formative years. Somewhere along the way, a caretaker may have failed you in one way or another. We will dive deeper soon, but know you can be abused or coddled into NPD. It is not your fault, but the cards you were dealt, and you have to take responsibility.

There is the temptation to go the positive route and think of NPD as the next stage in evolution; that having empathy is a bug not a feature. If you ever want to improve, you have to let this notion go. Your NPD might have been there to protect you at times, and there are positives to it. If you are more overt and confident, you go for opportunities because the idea of failure is inconceivable. But the drawbacks for most of you outweigh the benefits. If that weren't the case, you probably would not have picked up this book.

Lastly, narcissism does not *necessarily* make you evil or a broken person. Your actions and what you put into the world are the primary determinant. Society's relationship with narcissism is a funny one. Some narcissistic traits are coveted so long as it is not called narcissism. However, pride is one of the oldest sins, and in fiction, it is one of the easiest ways to show that a person is terrible. It is also almost always a fatal flaw and is diametrically opposed to the Everyman hero. As children, we are taught to root against narcissists and take glee when they fall down a cliff or get eaten by a pack of hyenas in our favorite movies.

The Public Price of the Spotlight

While science sought to understand narcissism, the media has done its best to pathologize to the point that it would make Freud blush. Cartoons like *The Animaniacs* would have their antagonist be the subject of mockery and sometimes physical violence for the crime of taking themselves a bit too seriously. When shows like Popeye had a confident show off of a protagonist, they balanced it by making this character handsome, getting the girl, and making their antagonist a bigger, uglier narcissist.

Content for adults also does people with narcissistic traits no favors. The narcissist is always the butt of the joke, especially when they are not the main antagonist. They are either too stupid to create actual conflict or an obstacle that needs to be overcome and who is never allowed to learn and grow, thanks to the horrors of syndicated television needing the characters to remain static.

If the content is based on real stories like true crime, then a criminal has every action that can be considered selfish on display. This circumstantial behavior is trotted out with a stone-cold narrator, creepy pictures getting their colors inverted, and unsettling music. While selfish behavior is morally wrong, it does not equate to being a monster, but it's that egoistic behavior that is used to fuel the audience's emotions from the start. These shows know that narcissism is the easiest way to make a person unsympathetic instead of, you know, the actual crime they committed.

It's not that criminals don't deserve scorn or an honest accounting of their lives, but to use a character flaw we are all guilty of to some degree for sensationalism is a problem. It plants the seed that all people with narcissistic traits are time bombs of misery waiting to happen creating a self-fulfilling prophecy. When a child does something deemed selfish, their behavior might not just be corrected. Instead, a less than effective adult conflates poor behavior with being a bad kid. Children internalize this feedback and, while some might pivot to the opposite direction, others might double down because if people already see you as evil, then what is the point of being good?

There is still a stigma around having mental health issues, but there is a callousness when it comes to NPD. When bad things happen to narcissists in public, the public relishes in the meltdown because it feels deserved. If you know anything about YouTube drama (don't leave;

there is a point here), you might remember what is now collectively called Dramageddon. The year is 2020, and we are all locked in our houses and have much free time to indulge in social media. Suddenly there are mutterings on Twitter about a scandalous video about to drop.

First, we should meet our characters. James Charles is a makeup influencer and an all-around insufferable human being. He became famous as a teenager and quickly went from middle-class nobody to a millionaire content creator. He had young fans worldwide, stroking his ego and telling him his makeup and techniques made him a god among peasants.

Then there is Tati Westbrook, another makeup influencer known for her aura of maturity and also James' mentor. She not only had her own makeup company, but she also sold vitamins under her brand. Their friendship soured when James endorsed a competitor's vitamins. While petty, this genuinely hurt her and left her vulnerable to the machinations of two of the worst people who ever had an internet platform to influence young people, Jeffery Star and Shane Dawson.

At this point, these two were at the top of their game and were known as being dramatic but ultimately entertaining and good-natured people (even though there was clear evidence to the contrary in hindsight). Jeffery Star also had his own makeup line, and the younger, more popular James Charles was his direct competitor. Shane Dawson hoped to ride on Starr's coattails and come out with his own makeup pallet, as makeup launches can rake in tens of millions of dollars in a single drop. So, they concocted a scheme in a plot to knock James Charles down several pegs.

They convinced Tati to release a video called "Bye Sister," where she explained how she was cutting ties with James because he was a predator who preyed on straight young men (more often than not, teenagers) and pressured them into a physical relationship. To say people ate it up is an understatement. Watching someone whose ego could not get any higher crash and burn was cathartic.

James Charles was metaphorically locked in the stocks in the town square while the townspeople threw tomatoes at him. The video was seen millions of times in 24hours, it was the height of Twitter discussion, and there was a movement to unsubscribe from James' channel. People were hosting watch parties on SocialBlade which showed his subscriber count in real-time. He lost nearly three million subscribers after the video.

Through a complicated and stupid series of events, James was vindicated when Tati revealed that Jeffery Starr and Shane Dawson manipulated her. It turns out that Charles did have a predilection for sending illicit pictures to teenage boys on the internet, but at the time, the public felt so used by the trio that they turned all three of them on a dime. Jeffery Starr had his past plastered on the internet showing him to be a sexist, racist, manipulative puppet master. After some digging, Shane Dawson's reputation of being an empathetic, humble, and harmless maker of poorly edited documentaries was shattered when his past of being an overall creep to children and animals was gathered and went viral on Twitter. Tati's reputation was ruined, and she lost her image as an unproblematic, unbiased voice of reason in such a little world. It was the trio's turn to get tomatoes hurled at them (Smokey Glow, 2021).

If you are a narcissist, people will remember it if you unapologetically treated them like shit. They may not say it out loud, but they will sit recumbent in their chair sipping a cocktail when you are at your lowest point. Without even knowing it, you may have burned every bridge you have.

The World is Working Against You (Kind of)

If you feel like narcissism is a modern phenomenon, you are not entirely wrong. The increasing complexity of our society and rise of capitalism can make a person fool themselves into believing they can be royalty, then lashing out when they realize it's an illusion. The rise of the family annihilator lends credence to this theory. These are killers that snap and kill their spouse and the majority of their children. These are mostly men who are fueled by:

- Economic motivations
- Self -righteousness
- Disappointment
- Anomic or financial motivations

- Paranoia

Before, people were content with living simple lives and providing for their families, despite a humble lifestyle. The modern world and economy can send a person spiraling if there is tangible proof that they are not living up to standards, be it their own or those of society. Despite the fact that most people don't have to worry about getting their arm ripped off in a thresher, work is more stressful than ever. Parents can work multiple jobs, scrap and save and still have nothing to show for it. These parents see their families as extensions of themselves and therefore feel entitled to put an end to it.

Let's Be Upfront: There is a Long Road Ahead

You are on the right track because you would not be reading this if you were not curious about another way of life. Unfortunately, there is no sugar coating here; people with NPD face many challenges with therapy that can end in self-sabotage. The process is long and awkward, and you might dive into crevices of your mind you have not touched since you were in knee socks. You have to go in with an open mind and patience for both your provider and yourself.

You might have successfully found a provider and made an appointment, but once you sit in that chair and realize what you have gotten yourself into, the old defense mechanisms come out to play. Therapists describe NPD as a challenge because therapy is inherently a collaborative and vulnerable process–two things that narcissists struggle with. You must be willing to let go of control and let a person in authority map out all your issues before you fix them. It's one thing knowing that something is off, but to hear it spelled out by a stranger with a diploma hanging on the wall is humbling, to say the least.

Clients may shut down during sessions or quit altogether, which is the provider's best-case scenario. Other times they may lash out and seek to hurt their therapist in the same way they feel like they are being attacked. One phenomenon is called transference, where the patient depersonalizes their emotions and transfers them to the provider. This is quite normal in sessions, but it can be taken a step further when the emotion is negative. Suddenly, if you think you are being picked on, you might start retaliating by picking on the therapist, who is just doing their job. You might call their practice a scam, start questioning their credentials, or tell them they should do everyone a favor and throw their license in a shredder. It's all an effort to experience the emotions in a way that doesn't damage the ego. Experienced therapists are well aware of this and are usually good at weaving through the punches (Zalman et al., 2019).

Transference can be beneficial if the therapist knowingly uses it as a tool. It might be the only way a therapist can see under the hood if a client is particularly guarded. This gives them a place to start in the client-therapist relationship. The provider can also ask follow-up questions and make clients reflect on their emotions (Poonam Sachdev, 2021).

Some therapists, through inexperience or just not being suited to the profession, can experience countertransference. This is when the provider takes the bait and responds to the client's needling. They start to take the jabs personally, and the provider now becomes psychologically exhausted. It can result in unprofessional behaviors and irreparable damage to the working relationship.

Since NPD is antithetical to the typical therapy experience, you and the therapist must be honest about progress. You might grow frustrated with slow progress, and your therapist might not be the right fit. While breaking ties with your provider is your prerogative, be honest about why this has become an option. Is it because the therapist is not providing you with tools to cope, is coddling you, or hears your diagnosis and stares at you like a cornered animal—or is it because you are having a mirror shone in your face and feel uncomfortable?

Your therapist might redirect your gripes with your past concerning current circumstances. You and your therapist can only work with what you can control. You cannot change the past, so blaming your parents after every hardship would waste both your time. Focus on yourself and make peace with being uncomfortable. It should also be noted that your therapist can fire you if they feel like they will not get anywhere with you by proceeding with treatment. If you have been fired from multiple therapists, some self-reflection might be in order.

Key Takeaways

- Narcissistic Personality Disorder (NPD) is characterized by self-centered thoughts and behaviors, a need for attention, and a sense of grandiosity.

- NPD is diagnosed based on a specific set of criteria by a professional.

- The biological causes of narcissism are still being studied, but research suggests that genetic factors and environmental influences, such as growing up in a narcissistic household, can contribute to its development.

- NPD can have physical health consequences like increased heart rates and higher cortisol levels, which can lead to heart disease and chronic stress.

- NPD can be comorbid with other mental health disorders, such as eating disorders, borderline personality disorder (BPD), anxiety, depression, and addiction. Each of these comorbidities presents unique challenges and requires comprehensive treatment approaches and an experienced professional.

- Narcissism is stigmatized in society, and its media portrayal can perpetuate misconceptions. We must avoid using the term loosely and turning it into a weapon.

- Seeking therapy for NPD can be challenging due to the inherent vulnerabilities and mandatory collaborative nature of the process. Clients with NPD may resist, and counter transfer in therapy sessions, making it crucial to find an experienced therapist and maintain open communication.

THE INNER CHILD OF A NARCISSIST

"No matter how socially skilled an extreme narcissist is, he has a major attachment dysfunction. The extreme narcissist is frozen in childhood."

- SAMUEL LOPEZ DE VICTORIA

As we have established, narcissists can be made by their childhood. Whether it be by the whip or being smothered, a child's world can be irreparably affected by ill-suited adults. The first step to healing and becoming more than this condition is recognizing what happened and letting it go. You cannot let these experiences define your personality. This does not mean you ignore it; quite the opposite, you accept it and recognize it has no control over you.

What Your Childhood Did to Your Thought Process

Children remember everything, as much as adults don't want to admit it. Every action, slip-up, and response is etched into their soul and informs the adult they will grow into. It doesn't even need to be outright abuse, nor does every child respond the same to every action. Genetic predisposition, birth order, gender, and culture play a part. Some kids can endure rough stuff and still emerge as functional adults.

To clearly illustrate this point, we can look at Zuko and Azula from *Avatar the Last Airbender*. In the show, they were the crowned prince and princess of the totalitarian Fire Nation that already completed one genocide and was prepping another under their father, Fire Lord Ozai. Both were groomed from birth to become ruthless soldiers and royalty by their fathers, but thanks to their personalities, Ozai profoundly affected them in different ways.

Zuko, despite being the firstborn son, was deemed a disappointment. He did not have the natural ruthlessness or talent in fire bending that his father craved. Zuko was a sensitive child especially compared to his younger sister Azula. While Zuko was, in his words, "lucky to be born," Azula was "born lucky." She had a fire in her eyes from birth; she was brilliant, talented, ruthless, and a born leader, everything Zuko wasn't.

Even as children, Ozai knew he would pass over Zuko in favor of his daughter. Ozai was openly ashamed of Zuko, and as he grew into a teenager, he ignored him and, at the first opportunity he got, mutilated and banished him on a journey he deemed impossible–capturing the Avatar. Meanwhile, he doted on Azula, showed her off, and reinforced her growing ego, which he saw as a strength.

In the series, Zuko shows the qualities of being a vulnerable narcissist. He was controlling over his team, condescending, refused to believe that even his loving Uncle Iroh could understand him, and hunted a group of children literally across the globe for one single-minded purpose, capturing the Avatar and restoring not only his honor but his father's respect for him.

On the other hand, Azula grew into a more outwardly malignant narcissist, albeit with shades of vulnerability thrown in at the end. She was comfortable in her station as a princess. She knew she was beautiful, powerful, and reveled in making even her friends afraid of her. She was also a perfectionist, which paid off in making her a powerful fire bender and one of the few who create lightning (a skill so dangerous, the bender cannot afford to have any doubt or distractions in their mind). In moments of insecurity, while Zuko responded with extreme anger and hostility, Azula would mock and belittle until she felt she had the upper hand. This is evidenced when even as a child, Azula roughly pushed her best friend Ty-Lee down for the crime of being able to complete a cartwheel sequence that she had fumbled earlier.

Azula didn't engage with the mission to hunt down Zuko (then confirmed alive) to make her father proud. She deemed her older brother and uncle as an embarrassment to the family. She considered it fun to hunt down her family and our heroes to more corners of the earth. Her charm, skill, and tactics eventually led to the capture of the once impenetrable Earth kingdom capital by turning its private army to her side and even teaming up with Zuko (by manipulating his need for approval) to deal a near-fatal blow to the Avatar.

These two characters come to a crossroads in the final season. Zuko is ultimately saved by his realization that the fire nation was cruel enough to enact another genocide and the positive influences in his life. First was his Uncle Iroh, a person he has done nothing but push away for the entire series culminating in letting him be taken prisoner. He realized that his uncle was more of a father than Ozai. He trained him, cared for him, and even joined him on his journey so he could have some support during a traumatizing time. It took a while to sink in, but his lessons on inner peace, finding the bright side of life, and seeking to do good finally became clear to Zuko.

There was also the influence of Team Avatar. People that, by all accounts, should have hated him repeatedly showed him mercy and eventually let their guard down enough to let him help. They were a model for a functional family, something Zuko had never had.

Finally, there was his mother, Ursa. Before she disappeared (it's a long story) when he was ten, she was the only source of warmth in Zuko's life. She reassured him of his bending, taught him to be gentle, and did a lot to protect him from Ozai's coldness and cruelty. That person was still inside Zuko, but after her disappearance, only having his father's influence was buried in bitterness and sadness. One thing to note is that Azula did not have the same relationship with her mother as Zuko. Because Ozai's influence on Azula was apparent from a very young age, Ursa became unsettled and even a bit frightened by her daughter, who favored fighting over playing and lit a doll her uncle gifted her on fire just because she didn't like it. This was not lost on Azula, who remarked to her friends, "My mother thought I was a monster". It was clear that she held some resentment over how easily she loved Zuko but struggled with her. Although she quickly followed it up with, "She was right, of course, but it still hurt."

Azula would not fare as well as her brother at the end of the series. Her worldview started to crack, and her sanity along with it. Unbeknownst to her, she had an extreme fear of rejection from her mother's rejection of her. She kept her friends and enemies in line with fear, as it was her only card to play. She may have been a captivating military leader, but she was not exactly a social butterfly. Fear worked very well for her up until a point. Her friends betrayed her because they refused to watch her kill Zuko, their friend since childhood.

This quickly unraveled into paranoia as she thought everyone would try and betray her. The final straw was when her father rejected her in his mission to destroy the Earth Kingdom, essentially electing to leave her in the car while he attended to business. She felt as low as Zuko, and she could not have that. She cracked, and her vulnerability ultimately led to her defeat at the hand of the brother and enemies she had looked down on until now.

Narcissism can be born of early dysfunction in the home. We think of a dysfunctional home as one with yelling, substance abuse, and physical violence, but that is not always the case. Dysfunction can also look like neglect and a swing in the opposite direction, like helicopter parenting or spoiling a child. Either way, each of these can leave deep emotional scars that the child will unfairly have to be the one to deal with. They can rise above and break the cycle or live their life ruled by it.

Neglect

Being a good person isn't just a matter of individual choice. In his theory of virtue ethics, Aristotle posited that we should strive to create virtuous communities. It's not just that having a community of ethical people is good; it also fosters the ability to propagate better people than those without such a community. Say you have two twins separated at birth. One goes to a virtuous family, and the other to a dysfunctional one. It's not that one twin was evil, and one was good as they grew up. The twin in the dysfunctional family never has a chance because they are in an environment that punishes virtuous behavior and rewards selfish behavior with survival.

When discussing neglect, we don't mean a child is starving or cold. Neglect, in this case, means a lack of emotional connection and attention while all physical needs are being met. This can apply to parents who don't necessarily mean to hurt or torment their kids but are just so overwhelmed or self-centered that they have lost the plot on why someone would bring a kid into the world in the first place. Parents who only know how to show love by throwing money at a kid and providing for their basic needs fall into this category.

As mammals are genetically programmed to remain with and depend on our parents for a long time, certain expectations are ingrained in our DNA. It's not enough for babies to be fed and changed; they need to know they can depend on their parents for safety and, most importantly, love. Even monkeys show this level of dependence. When given a choice between a cold robot that will simply feed it or a soft furry body with nothing more to offer than a simulated heartbeat, a monkey would rather starve than not have that approximation of its mother's comfort (Harlow et al., 1965).

Childhood neglect creates narcissism because somewhere along the way, a child figures out that they can only depend on themselves for soothing. Even at a few months old, a baby has a bag of tricks to engage with their caregiver. They smile and laugh and need the recipient to acknowledge that. If not, they cry; if they are still ignored, they cease crying and start chewing or rocking. It doesn't even need to be outward neglect, such as leaving the kid in a room all day and refusing to deal with them. If you comfort a child but are also distracted by a smartphone, your baby is not getting the interaction they crave. Like the baby monkey, it is more important for them to feel secure than meet their needs for long-term development. This can mess with crucial social development that can impact an individual's personality until adulthood because the parent cannot be trusted to show love.

Ultimately, you may end up with a child who does not care about engaging with others because they never learned how or had it reinforced as a waste of energy. You can also have someone who will swing in the other direction and dedicate themselves to receiving any validation, even if it is distracting or harmful. They might become disruptive in class or lash out because it is the only way they know how to get someone to respond to them.

You may also end up with someone who becomes addicted to the idea of finding unconditional love. They may become anxious and paranoid that a person they care about is slipping through their fingers and will threaten, lie, and manipulate to keep them in the palm of their hand (Karyl McBride, 2011).

Abuse

Abusive parents create an environment where the child can never feel safe or secure. While an emotionally neglected child may have a roof over their head and food on the table, an abused child may go hungry or cold on top of being abused. They learn the above lessons, except on steroids, because they are shown that the only way to deal with something is by yelling at it, hitting it, or punishing it. We aren't born with a manual called "How to be a functional human" etched in our brains; we learn from examples whether it is good or not.

Narcissistic parents who have multiple children to abuse often have techniques to keep their children emotionally isolated from each other. One of those is pitting the children against each other by having a "golden child" and a "scapegoat child." The golden child will often escape punishment, be given special treatment, and might receive the part of the parent that wants to live vicariously through them. Parents might even go out of their way to fill their heads with the idea that their siblings hate them and that they can only depend on their parents.

Then there is the "scapegoat," the black sheep, or the unfavorite. This child will never be good enough to win their parents' affection. Every problem in the family's lives is because of them. This child gets the brunt of physical and emotional abuse, receives nothing but hand-me-downs, and systematically destroys their self-esteem. This dynamic has an extra twist of the knife because the child sees that the parent can give (their form of twisted) affection. The child will chase that love but will learn that they will never receive it from the narcissistic parent. Instead, they have to be constantly on guard not to shine too bright or amass too many resources because the parent might see it as a threat to their golden child and, therefore, themselves. The parent can create that self-fulfilling prophecy as the scapegoat child may resent the golden child because they did not stop the abuse or help out when they could. This might not be entirely wrong, especially if the golden child spell lasts into adulthood and they double down on the behavior and do not see it for its abuse. However, the golden child is also a victim and should not be solely blamed for any actions they did not take as a child. It's the adults in the house that failed (Heidi Butler, 2022).

If you have ever seen the show *Dance Moms,* you have seen this firsthand with Maddie Ziegler and her teacher Abby Lee Miller. Maddie was an exceptionally talented dancer because she had great musicality and was a quick learner. Abby Lee gave her all the best dances, costumes, and attention, constantly criticized the class for not being as good as her, and even told her student that everyone else was jealous of her. Only after the show ended did Ziegler realize she was also a victim, even though her abuse looked different from the other students. She suffered extreme anxiety and was terrified of failing her teacher if she got any less than first place. She felt that she needed to be perfect at all times, and it took getting some distance from her old dance teacher to see what was going on. She cut off the woman who was the most critical adult in her life and never looked back.

Coddling

Another slightly less acknowledged way narcissists are created is by doting on them incessantly. It goes well beyond teaching a child confidence and healthy competition. That would imply that the parent gave the kid the tools they need so they know that they can handle losing. They feel secure because they know they have a support system and know not to catastrophize whenever they come short. Smothering can look like:

- Telling the child how great they are constantly, even if they haven't earned lavish praise.

- Putting down other children to lift the child up.

- Always giving into a child's demands.

- Putting sky-high expectations in the child's head from a young age.

- Doing everything for the child to the point where they rely on the parent for basic needs into adolescence, and even adulthood.

- Never letting the child face consequences for misdeeds.

- Venting to and treating the child as a therapist.

While this is a much better life for a kid than having an outright abused childhood, this kid is still being failed by their parents. This kid may be unable to take care of themselves, cannot cope with failure, and has their head filled with grandiose dreams but no sense of accountability. When they grow up and move on beyond their bubble, they are in for a rude awakening when they realize they can't do anything, and peers have no patience for an adult who is well behind everyone else. Now this person has two paths; they can realize that they have a lot of catching up to do, or they lean into what their parents told them, that they are unique and everyone else is the problem.

Several real monsters come from a combination of both smothering and abusive houses, often with the father being a domineering, violent force, and a mother overcorrecting. The smotherer is often in an impossible situation with an abusive partner. However, coping mechanisms involving the child can have grave consequences even if they didn't mean for that to happen. The smotherer in this dynamic comes from the fact that they realize their life and self-esteem have reached a low point. A parent with low self-esteem might project their dreams on a child in the most maladaptive way possible. This is when they ensure that the kid is never challenged by any adult outside the house, is showered with compliments, and might be told that they will be the one to save the family by succeeding in life. Because abusive relationships often involve isolation, the only person the smotherer can vent to is the kid. A child who still has to raise their hand to go to the bathroom is stuck hearing their parent, a person they are supposed to see as their protector, talk about dysfunction that goes well beyond their head or their emotional intelligence. They now have to take on the parent role of being the rock and a source of assurance for an adult, creating a flipped dynamic between parent and child.

This can be taken even further if the child tries to get in between the abuser and the other parent. This child now sees themself as their parents' hero. It must be emphasized that this parentification of a child is not part of a functional household. Kids can rise above this and become strong adults, albeit through less-than-ideal circumstances. Other times, this dynamic creates a person who, from a very young age, saw themselves as larger than life and in a position of power as a protector. The second they hit the real world, they realize that none of that applies to work or friends, and they were never socialized to accept this. Suddenly they are no longer mom's unique little child who can walk on water. They are mortal, and that break in ego has created some severe monsters through the years (Jack Jones, 2000).

Lessons from Monsters 1
The Dysfunctional Menendez Family

Before we get into this real-world story round, we should clarify a few things. For one, these people are not monsters because they are narcissists; they are people whose narcissism drove them to do monstrous things. Also, some of these people have never formally been diagnosed, but according to people in their life, they had some narcissistic tendencies.

With that, let's go back to the magical time of the 1980s. Jose Menendez was a Cuban immigrant who was at the height of success. He had a successful career as a producer, was married, wealthy, and had two sons, Eric and Lyle Menendez. It was everything Jose had dreamed of as he worked from floating to the United States to escape the Castro regime to being a man of influence and status. He wanted his sons to have the same tough-as-nails cutthroat attitude (his mantra was literally "cheat, steal, lie"), as he felt it was the only way they would be successful. Jose was an abrasive, micromanaging menace to his sons. He would only allow them to play one sport and would scold his sons in front of their friends if they dared to play soccer instead of their assigned sports of tennis and swimming. He would drill them on current events, host motivational seminars, and force them to recite a minute-long creed every morning. Still, others maintained that the boys were given everything and should have been on a shorter leash. Both of these can be true with a permissive mother and a dictator of a father, so it was no surprise the impact that this parenting had.

To say that his sons did not meet his expectations was an understatement. Eric and Lyle were spoiled kids who regularly threw temper tantrums and were nowhere near the cunning businessmen Jose wanted them to be. On top of that, Lyle had a delicate constitution. He would wet the bed into his adolescence (where he would be forced to eat breakfast with his soiled sheets on the table) and lose his hair before he turned 18. One son didn't attend college and the other got kicked out of Princeton after a single semester. Jose had failed as a father and created two children with an extreme amount of entitlement and resentment. Rumor has it he was going to cut them out of the will. The money their father had was the only card they had to play–this could not stand.

In 1989, Eric and Lyle would shoot their parents in the face with a shotgun. Even though their rage was directed at Jose, they also elected to shoot their mother because that would be more merciful than her life as a widow. They managed to keep the police off their scent through a theatrical display of grief for now. The boys then shopped for new watches, cars, and a restaurant before their parents' bodies were cold. The insane spending raised alarms, and since the boys could not keep their mouths shut about the crime, they were swiftly arrested and became the center of the very trial that put court TV on the map.

Depending on your opinion, the boys sank even lower by alleging that Jose was not only emotionally abusive, but sexually abusive as well. Several family members corroborated that story. Public opinion is split on the motives and whether or not the boys deserved jail. They gave a harrowing account of abuse on the stand. However, this story did not come to light until the trial three years after their arrest. There is also the fact that the family had about 15 million reasons in the form of inheritance to ensure the boys walked. The money, for all intents and purposes, would poof out of existence if they lost the case–which is exactly what happened. The brothers were sentenced to life for the murders thanks to a half-baked scheme and the inability to not flex their fortune (Robert Rand, 2018).

Internal Conversations

When a person is raised in a narcissistic environment, their tool kit is based on one thing: control. These are people that grew up in an environment not only lacking in love, but in agency. There are a couple of paths here. They can vow never to lose control again. They perpetuate the same cycle where they make someone else feel just as low as them, so they become putty in a narcissist's hands. The other path is to double down on not having any control and seek someone to always take care of them. They use similar techniques but are more insidious because of the power dynamic at play.

The overt narcissist doesn't need to pretend. All parties involved know who is in charge and who has the power. The covert narcissist has a bit of a dance to pull off. They need the other person to see them as weak but not weak enough that they have any sort of upper hand. This is where a narcissist will use one of their more effective tools: guilt. Their power lies in their ability to guilt-trip anyone into never leaving them. The narcissist can act weak and defenseless but still in complete control because they pick out kind, empathetic, and often naive people to target in their scheme.

Accepting Your Past

You must accept your past for what it is: an explanation of your current predicament and not an excuse. You are a person who can make choices and can ultimately choose not to continue the cycle. Will this cure your narcissism? Of course not, but it will help you see the bigger picture. You seek power from others because it was never afforded to you; you seek validation because it is something that you were not taught to give to yourself. You have effectively projected your entire history onto other people in an attempt to cope with it, and it will destroy your relationships. Be honest with yourself. Do you see others as human beings with wants, desires, and the ability to make their own choices? Or a possession you have to guard like a kid with a new toy on a playground?

No one argues that you did not have a hard life or are not a victim. You are a different person than you might have been had you not had such a sordid past. It's okay to feel resentment, anger, and disappointment as you mourn someone you could have been. However, you may be dealing with self-loathing in a way your mind can handle by punishing others instead of yourself. The sooner you recognize your harmful behaviors as maladaptive coping, the better.

Schema Therapy to Heal Your Inner Child

We know that our childhood doesn't just leave fingerprints on our adult self. It informs how we approach being an adult, and those experiences can either be steel reinforcements built by good parents and influences, or scars that we are constantly paying for. If you want to cut the bullshit and get to these core beliefs, schema therapy might be for you.

Schemas are the patterns we use to interact with the world built from childhood. If your formative years were spent in a bubble of abuse and manipulation by people you are supposed to trust, you might have no concept that people can be inherently good. Your defenses and poor socialization can destroy any positive relationship that enters your life (Dieckmann & Behary, 2015). It's like trying to receive a hug when you are also a cactus. Someone may try, but they will never last long.

Using a combination of Cognitive Behavioral Therapy (CBT) and psychodynamic theories (how our unconscious mind can affect us) with an emphasis on attachment theory, narcissists might finally learn what it means to have a healthy relationship using these steps.

- **Schema Awareness:** To hone in on the exactly affected schemas, a therapist may try guided imagery, role-playing, and exploring childhood memories. The client may be unaware or unwilling to divulge specific memories and thought patterns. This gives the therapist a more honest look at the client's current mind frame and pain points.

- **Cognitive Restructuring**: Clients now know what their schemas are, and they can work on identifying what triggers their maladaptive behaviors as adults. They must recognize them for what they are and work to reframe these triggers into something they can manage without damaging relationships or losing their cool.

- **Emotional Regulation**: Schema therapy acknowledges that while emotions are dysregulated, they exist and must be dealt with, not buried. Now that they have identified these triggers, clients can work with distress *tolerance*. This is where the client is slowly exposed to their triggers so they can learn to let them roll off their back instead of having an outburst or letting it fester.

- **Behavioral Change**: Therapists will teach and reinforce new coping behaviors for the client. Until now, coping has included grandiose behavior, attention seeking, or substance abuse. Things like self-care, mindfulness, and setting achievable goals are among the strategies that are taught.

- **Healing the Inner Child**: Childhood is where we learn how to navigate and meet our emotional needs, whether seeking support or learning to self-soothe. The client needs to learn not only compassion for others, but for themselves. Through nurture and a bit of parenting, the therapist guides the client through these skills and milestones that they may have been robbed of.

- **Limited Parent Relationship**: The therapist takes on a parental role for the client. This must be somewhat limited to maintain professional integrity, but the client needs to learn how to trust a supportive quasi-authority figure. The therapist provides empathy, validation, offers advice, and a source of support and security. All the things the client may have lacked with their actual parental figure.

This is not a twelve-week program with a therapist. Schema therapy can last a long time since undoing patterns set in childhood is not a trivial task. Still, with the right motivation and a growing sense of self-awareness, a narcissist can begin the healing process and become a better person (Bamelis et al., 2014).

Key Takeaways

- Narcissists can be created by their childhood experiences of abuse or neglect.

- Recognizing and letting go of past experiences is the first step towards breaking free from narcissistic thought patterns.

- Coddling a child excessively can also lead to narcissistic tendencies, as it creates entitlement, a warped view of the world, and the inability to take accountability or experience failure.

- Healing from narcissism involves accepting the past, understanding core beliefs, restructuring thoughts and behaviors, emotional regulation, and healing the inner child through therapy.

DEALING WITH THE SIN OF PRIDE

"Narcissists would rather lie and humiliate you than to admit that they were in the wrong."

- MITTA XININDLU

There is nothing wrong with holding your head up high and being sure of your abilities. However, if you are a narcissist, you have most likely taken your ego up several levels. Pride that becomes maladaptive can develop in a few ways. As we discussed, it can be a coping mechanism for trauma and familial dysfunction. It can also emerge if a person suddenly gains a lot of power, especially when young. When you are powerful, you are never challenged and therefore decide that you have learned all you can. In John Lennon's case, he was 16 when he sang for millions of adoring fans and became one of the most recognizable people on the planet. That changed brain chemistry, and he was still a child.

More people are starting to realize that Lennon got a bit obnoxious in later years. The man once the voice for the peace and love era of the 60's had grown into your typical grandiose, mega-wealthy celebrity. He would say things (that were shocking at the time) like the Beatles were bigger than Jesus, and for a guy who sang about a world without possessions, he sure had a lot of them in his Manhattan penthouse. This was on top of beating his first wife, discarding his first son like trash, and blighting the world with Yoko. Some might say that becoming that famous that young stunted Lennon's development and angered some of his fans (we'll come back to this).

How Ego Can Destroy You

Trying to Grasp a Mirage

When narcissists develop their image, they often don't think about the work it takes to maintain it. It's so easy to say things about you, your past, and your abilities, and as we have learned through this series of books, keeping track of a lie is insanely difficult. Unless you have a laminated card with every lie or exaggeration you have ever told, you will probably contradict yourself at some point. This is magnified by the fact that it's not just that narcissists forget or overlook their mistakes; they are highly aware of and very critical of them (Mück et al., 2023). So, you can't help but make this web and you will know the second you get caught in it, making for some intense anxiety and emotional dysregulation when you realize that you may have just painted yourself into a corner.

So, what do you do? Since narcissists cannot cope with failure or their shattered image, they double down. It's as if Australia released venomous cobras to deal with their mistake of releasing cane toads. You will end up with another lie to keep track of. You know this in the back of your head, but the need to maintain your ego is so strong that you start pathological lying. When lying becomes pathological, there is only one rule–it must serve to paint you as a hero or a victim at any cost. There doesn't need to be logic or planning, and it doesn't even need to serve any concrete purpose.

There is some debate regarding the classification of pathological lying and compulsive lying. Some think they can be used interchangeably. Others feel pathological lying should be classified as a consistent and conscious attempt to warp reality. This person can still become delusional if they believe their own lies. Compulsive lying is just lying for the sake of lying. For our purposes, we are going to use the term *pathological lying*.

Let's say someone talks about how they played varsity soccer in high school. A narcissist who cannot be one-upped might counter with a lie, saying they also played varsity soccer and were part of a winning team. This lie was utterly pointless; nothing tangible was gained by telling it. It isn't a lie to try to earn a scholarship; all that happened was the narcissist felt like they were on top for 30 seconds before the topic of conversation changed. But you commit to the lie, and soon the lies pile up like a ball and chain you must carry around.

Hanging On to Delusion

So, you are caught in your web of lies, each more complicated than the last but it's okay because only you know the truth. You have to fool everyone else, and it will be fine–right? Unfortunately, you must remember that people are more observant than you think, especially if they are suspicious or don't like you. So, now you have to tell the lie and become the lie. If you lost your job, guess who will be hiding at their local library for eight hours a day and start taking out credit card debt: you are! Did you tell people you know martial arts, but the closest you came to a dojo was watching a Jackie Chan movie? Well, now you have to sign up for classes. You will live your life being pulled by the lies you told on the fly rather than how you want.

Chasing a mirage instead of honing your natural talents and potential will fast-track you into a life of unhappiness. Have you ever met someone who picked a college major because of potential wealth and status without thinking about whether they like it or are even suited to it? These types believe they will be a hero by pursuing a medical degree but get filtered out by an undergraduate chemistry class. Wanting something and being the right fit for something are two different things. If you are pursuing something challenging, you must be fully aware of what you are getting into and have reasons other than potential wealth. There are easier ways to make money.

History, media, and our personal lives are filled with people who went completely over their heads to fuel their egos. One particularly tragic example is Tupac Shakur. He was a rapper who stormed the world in the 1990's. The image he kept for himself was as a hard gangbanger who would not only climb to the top of the music industry but be a strongman in the East Coast-West Coast gang wars that were a part of that scene. The only issue was that his whole image was nothing more than hype.

Tupac had an undeniably rough childhood. However, he was never a gangbanger. He didn't sling drugs or shoot anyone to survive. He rapped and profited off of the life but was never actually in it. He would have been more concerned with the gang than singing if he had been. Still, he saw a ton of success to the point where he got to act in programs like *In Living Color* and *Above the Rim,* the role that planted the seeds that would doom him. It was at this premiere, where Tupac saw himself in the role of a gang leader, that Tupac's self-image and ideations were irreparably changed. He saw himself on a giant screen as everything he ever wanted to be. He was singing in a role where he did not have to pretend to be in the life. His close friends said he was never the same, and he chased that life further by surrounding himself with dangerous people so he could absorb it through affiliation.

Even with his new serious friends, Tupac was never really a gangster. He had claimed to have been shot five times and survived. However, most people said he shot himself once. His talents with a gun can also be called into question after getting into an altercation, and instead of shooting his opponent, he missed and accidentally shot and killed a six-year-old boy. Tupac was no criminal mastermind and was not cut out for gang life. That didn't change the fact that his close friends were hardened men.

Tupac had a chance to learn his lesson when he was convicted of being in a group that sexually brutalized a woman in his hotel room. Tupac is responsible for his role in this crime, but one has to wonder if it would have happened if his posse was filled with better people and not actual criminals who saw him as a way to access women. Tupac sold his soul to Satan, Suge Knight, to post bail. He signed a three-record contract with him to work off the money Suge had posted for his bail. You would think that becoming an indentured servant to one of hip hop's greatest monsters would cause Tupac to reevaluate his life. All it did was make him closer to Suge Knight and all the dangerous people he had at his beck and call.

Had Tupac stuck with acting, something he was clearly good at, he might have followed the same trajectory as Ice-Cube or Iced-Tea, a former rapper from the streets now entertaining the masses on *Law and Order* or classics like *Are We There Yet* (Ben Westhoff, 2017).

On September 13, 1996, Tupac was killed in a drive-by shooting after a Mike Tyson fight. The inciting incident was the attempted theft of a necklace by a Crips member earlier that year. Someone in Tupac's crew spotted the thief, and a brawl ensued. Later that night, it is widely believed that a Crips member named Orlando Anderson riddled the car Tupac was in with bullets, killing him. At 25 years old, with the whole world ahead of him, Tupac was dead over a necklace that wasn't even his. He had the talent and the charisma to go far in whatever endeavor he could imagine, but because he insisted on keeping up with his gangster image, he was dead, and the world would never know how far he could go (Greg Kading, 2011).

Blinded By Ambition

Sulley: Mike, I don't know a single scarer who can do what you do...You took a hopeless team, and made them champions... you think you're just okay?! You pulled off the biggest scare this school's ever seen!

Mike: That wasn't me.

Sully: You think I could have done that without you? Mike, you're not scary, not even a little, but you are fearless!

—Monsters University

Narcissism can cause some severe tunnel vision. You not only lack the self-awareness of the present, but you are so fixated on this grandiose version of yourself and how you don't measure up that you fail to see what's in front of you. One of the most dangerous things in this world is being less intelligent than you think. It leads to mistakes and being taken advantage of. Why? Because inevitably, someone savvy in what you are pretending to be will show up. You might not be able to help but brag about your pretend abilities, and there is no greater schadenfreude than proving a person wrong. Why live like this? Why not focus and tend to your actual talents? You can still be great; maybe it's not what you expected, but greatness is still attainable. The curse of the Forbes 30 Under 30 list would be avoided if these egomaniacs gained a little perspective on what they are good at.

We all remember Elizabeth Holmes. For those of you who need a reminder, she is the former CEO of the now-defunct Theranos, who touted her diagnostic machine as a revolution that could run multitudes of tests with a single finger prick. It was big talk as it could eliminate the need for painful blood draws and upend the juggernaut of Quest Diagnostics. Of course, it was all a lie that has been chronicled in numerous books, podcasts, documentaries, and television (don't be surprised if a Theranos stage adaptation is in the works). Holmes would not be going to jail if she realized a straightforward truth—she was never a scientist or an engineer. She only completed up to her sophomore year in college and had no practical or even classroom experience. She was a kid playing scientist and had not earned her stripes in the lab and contributed to the field.

What Elizabeth missed is that she is an insanely good salesperson. She sold this idea, backed by nothing but her hopes and dreams, to political giants such as Henry Kissinger, George Shultz, a few sitting members of Congress and presidential candidates, Walgreens, and experienced journalists. She could have made a comfortable living in the business and marketing side of biotechnology. Instead, she will be in jail for years because she could not let go of her unattainable dream (John Carreyrou, 2020).

Lessons From Monsters 2:
John List

If you want a front-row seat to holding onto a delusional fantasy for pride's sake, look no further than the family annihilation of the List family. John List was an incredibly repressed and religious man, impotently trying to raise the quintessential religious American family. Growing up with an abusive father and a manipulative mother, John was a compulsive rule follower and was set to live his life under his Southern religious teaching and suffocating environment. His father never showed him any affection, electing to call him "the boy" rather than the name he gave him. He never disobeyed his parents to the point he would not play with other children lest his mother scold him for getting his clothes dirty. His evangelical upbringing drilled a few things into his head:

- His work dictates a man's worth.

- The prosperity gospel, where wealth was proof that you have pleased God and poverty was evidence of sin.

- Accepting charity was akin to emasculation and not Christian (which is ironic considering actual Catholic doctrine).

- Straying from the church in any way was the fast track to spending eternity in a lake of fire.

Unfortunately, these values would create a pressure cooker in John's mind, especially when he started a family.

To say John List's married life was not what he imagined would be an understatement. He met the widow Helen List at (what else?) a church function. They (hypocritically) engaged in premarital sex, and John felt it would be a sin not to marry her. Unfortunately, Helen was not precisely the demure, obedient housewife that overly religious men of that time desired. Helen had contracted syphilis from her husband and did not receive treatment before the disease took root and ravaged her brain. She was prone to bouts of depression and impulsivity and was an all-around handful, especially to a tightwad like John. She would criticize him for his appearance and performance in the bedroom and compare him to her late husband, who died a war hero in front of his coworkers. To top it all off, she lied about the pregnancy, but since divorce was a sin, John was stuck with Helen and proceeded to raise a family who would go on to pay for every blow to their father's ego.

John List could be categorized as an Omic family annihilator, or someone who does what they do because of financial strain. The List family would expand to five kids, and the family, along with John's mother, would pick up and move to a mansion that they could not afford. John was an accountant, which he was good at, but as the business world changed in the '60s, he could not adapt.

While good with numbers, he was a terrible manager and an even worse salesman. He kept getting fired, and instead of telling his family what was going on, he would pretend to go to work and read the paper all day. Remember, taking charity was not the Christian thing to do, so John had to rush and find another job before the money ran out, taking less and less pay each time. The house had been triple mortgaged, and Helen would insist on the nicest clothes and furniture for the family.

The final straw was that he saw his entire family as a disappointment. They all started distancing themselves from the church, which included not attending mass and his daughter wearing a thin cotton T-shirt, breaking curfew, celebrating Halloween, and being a part of a high school theater group. John was at the end of his rope. His wife had emasculated him, he was failing as a father, a provider, and a Christian man, and he had lost control of his kids despite them being all-around decent children despite their parents. John's most immediate problem was money troubles; obviously, accepting welfare and making his family downsize was out of the question. Plus, John didn't want to solve his financial problems; by this time, his bitterness from how his life turned out seeped into his family; he hated his wife, resented his mother, and thought his kids were too far gone. If he just killed Helen and ran, without his influence the children would be tempted by Satan even faster, so leaving them alive was not an option.

In a bout of mental gymnastics that would win every Olympic gold medal, John reasoned that they still had a chance to get into heaven if he killed everyone. His financial problems would be over, his annoying family would be a funny memory, and he could start again. But what about the elephant in the room, you may ask, "Isn't murder the worst sin?"

Well, John thought of that, too; if you go to confession and ask God for forgiveness, you still get into heaven to have an awkward reunion with the people you murdered. John methodically planned out the murder, and over the entire day, he killed his whole family, with nearly all of them knowing that it was him pulling the trigger and snuffing them out.

While John was a crappy corporate employee, he was very good at planning and executing a murder. He stopped all deliveries to his house so no one would notice mail and newspapers piling up. He let the school know his children would not be attending, took emergency leave from his job, left the lights on so it would look like people were home, and finally, he turned down the thermostat so the bodies would rot slower and not cause a smell that would alert authorities. It's actually very difficult to get away with murder, but thanks to a lack of internet and all of his planning, he got away with all of this for 20 years.

While on the run, John List managed to keep a low profile. He became a short-order cook and moved into a trailer to support himself. Why poverty was acceptable for him and not his family is just an infuriating part of his ego run wild, especially since he was good at cooking in a high-paced kitchen. He eventually started dating again and again, draining another person financially to get back his white-collar accountant job.

Before he could go back to his murdering ways, though, he was caught only because the cold case was featured on America's most wanted. John List would spend 20 years in prison before dying a broken man (Joe Sharkey, 2018). John List is a cautionary tale about living up to an illusion built by your ego. This vision is so narrow you are blinded to other possibilities once you inevitably fall short. Instead of using all of your talents to reach some potential, you would rather hit self-destruct than break that fantasy.

Humility: The Antidote to Pride

Cognitive Behavioral Therapy

If you are seeking professional help, CBT may help you come down to earth. At its core, CBT is all about how a person's beliefs can influence their actions. It's not about stopping the behavior (like putting a shock collar on a dog and hoping it doesn't hop over the fence), it's about the reconstruction of your worldview, so you walk the walk and talk the talk. A person with narcissism can be dealing with a ton of cognitive distortions that can look like:

- **Black and white thinking:** Either everyone thinks you are fantastic, or everyone is plotting against you. This makes relationships, hobbies, and entire swathes of your life incredibly fragile. Either things are going perfectly, or it's broken and needs to be forcibly fixed or thrown away.

- **Magnification:** Narcissists can habitually focus on the detail they need to justify their worldview. They will also hang on to any perceived achievement and either inflate its importance or embellish facts—even the tiniest divergence of expected behavior. For example, a person saying with a flat tone that they enjoyed the dinner you cooked instead of saying it with a smile can set a narcissist off into their victim mentality.

- **Magical thinking:** This is the belief that everything will work out by the grace of the narcissist's intelligence, divine right, and everything that does not include the facts of the situation and taking into account other people's behaviors and opinions. This can make a narcissist extremely difficult to work with and lead to a ton of disappointment or mental gymnastics. It also makes it so the narcissist can never fail because only something entirely out of their control can mess with the natural order of getting what they want.

You can see how these distortions harm everyone, including the narcissist. CBT works on helping the narcissist see things for what they actually are. Just like it helps those with anxiety see that the world is not as dangerous as their fear tells them, it allows narcissists to see that the world does not revolve around them (Dr. Todd Grande, 2018).

CBT gives minimal leeway for a narcissist to take control. It emphasizes structure, gives homework, and as the therapist is the one who devises all of this, they are clearly in charge. It can be the perfect environment for someone to learn to give up some control and gain some perspective on how their brain interprets the world. You learn to challenge your beliefs. This does not mean you develop self-hatred; it means you are more realistic about your role in this world. Not everything is on your shoulders; you are allowed to relax without the weight of grandiose thinking.

CBT focuses on behaviors before addressing thought patterns, so therapy might initially feel a bit phony. The therapist knows that a selfish person may not be open to having their grandiose self-image challenged immediately. Instead, they try exercises so a person with NPD can get practice engaging in self-reflection and emotional regulation. Therapy will NOT look like this:

> *Client: It's all Becca's fault I got in trouble at work! I told her exactly how I needed this done, and she couldn't. Now the boss thinks I'm the incompetent one.*
>
> *Therapist: You sound incredibly frustrated, but at the wrong person. Did you ever consider your boss might be right?*

It will most likely look like this:

> *Therapist: That sounds like a frustrating situation. Let's look at the things we can control. In our previous sessions, you stated you were new to training subordinates. You even said you liked working with Becca. Could Becca have needed more training before taking on this responsibility? Are you happy with the amount of time you have been able to dedicate to training?*

Client: I guess I have been busy writing a proposal and haven't been able to monitor her progress as closely as I would have hoped.

Therapist: If you were your boss, who would you go to first, the subordinate employee or the staff member responsible for their training?

Client: I see your point.

The client may not be 100% convinced of what they are saying, but that is not the point. The goal is to get them used to introspection and taking responsibility, as well as appropriate control. Remember, the mother of mastery is repetition. Eventually, this practice will bleed into behaviors and thoughts naturally.

CBT can also be used to treat pathological lying. Constant bending or breaking of the truth can be seen as a maladaptive behavior. You cope with the fear of people looking down on you by making yourself look better, whatever the cost. CBT challenges your thought patterns, and the goal is to ultimately learn better behaviors. Recognizing when you will lie, slowing down, and realizing that it's okay if you don't always have the upper hand, even in the pettiest of situations, will keep you from getting caught in your web.

Key Takeaways

- Pride can quickly become maladaptive, especially when it is born from trauma or familial dysfunction.

- Narcissists often develop a web of lies to maintain their image, which can lead to anxiety.

- Pathological lying is a common trait of narcissists. It is an effort to maintain the upper hand no matter how petty the reason.

- Being caught in lies can lead to a loss of control and the need to snowball more lies to maintain the illusion.

- Chasing an unrealistic image can prevent individuals from honing their natural talents, ultimately leading to unfulfillment.

- People blinded by ambition tend to make mistakes and get taken advantage of.

- The antidote to pride is humility, and cognitive-behavioral therapy (CBT) can help individuals challenge their distorted beliefs, become self-aware, and delve in introspection to cultivate a more realistic worldview.

WHY IT IS IMPORTANT TO LEARN
WHEN ENOUGH IS ENOUGH

"Narcissism is voluntary blindness, an agreement
not to look beneath the surface."

- SAM KEEN

One way or another, narcissists feel entitled to both
material and more abstract things. Consumption is a
form of status that doesn't require grandiose
accomplishments, just access to a bank account. They
also cover the energy and attention of everyone around
them. This reaches its final form when the narcissist
starts to see a person not just as a source of validation,
but as a possession. They are repeatedly dehumanized
and, like toys, will be a source of release for a narcissist's
insecurity.

At its worst, a narcissist will punish their possession to
punish themselves and rationalize it as something foisted
upon them. This whole line of reasoning is a trap
because, thanks to the nature of narcissism and

humanity, it will never be enough. There is only so much you can accumulate or so much love you can receive, but if you are using it to fill something in your soul, it is impossible because it is like trying to fill a cracked cup. The core emotion of narcissism is fear, and if you start to perceive any loss of control or see someone else with more than you, that fear is fed, and the cup bottoms out again.

Coveting attention

A narcissist always needs to be the center of attention. Whether it was through a lack of positive reinforcement, self-esteem, or an environment with impossibly high standards, a narcissist never learns how to regulate their internal validation, nor do they understand what things society praises and what it doesn't.

Sometimes children who are born into neglectful or abusive environments only receive any sort of parental attention if they misbehave. Yes, it is in the form of physical or verbal abuse, but in a twisted way, it is an acknowledgment. A child will no longer feel gaslit into thinking they don't exist, and they will hang on to that feeling for dear life.

The Spell of Dehumanization

It is difficult to wring a person dry if you see them as a human first. That's why narcissists have this one simple trick. They regularly dehumanize the people around them to let the narcissist keep up the delusion that they are a good person. It's easy to justify bad behavior and impulses if you don't see the humanity in others. These aren't people with their own experiences and opinions. They, by default, agree with you; if they don't, you uncouple their humanity and make them deserving of scorn. People do this often with those they are attracted to or see as having an advantage.

> *He's so handsome; I'm sure he's a jerk to every woman he meets because they would put up with it.*
>
> *Ugh, I'm sure she's a slut who sleeps with a different guy every week.*
>
> *He didn't want to go out with me; he must be closeted to reject this.*
>
> *I'm sure they only promoted her to fill some quota.*
>
> *Life must be so easy for them!*

Rejection or failure can never be their fault or the result of being bested. It is some grand conspiracy against the narcissist. Since there is a level of insecurity about being unable to engage or measure up, they start making snap moral judgments or assumptions about this person. It is an effort to keep from getting rejected by beating the world to the punch. In its mildest form, it makes the narcissist judgmental; in its final form, people are lesser than others and are also toys for amusement.

As the Stanford Prison experiment showed, if you give a person a position of authority, they can quickly become a monster who revels in tormenting those underneath them. Some of it is a form of self-preservation. If you are faced with a force that can wipe you out, but you can hide behind someone else, most people would. However, this feeling of a lack of control is unsettling, so a person can make up reasons why they are being spared. If there was a serial killer on the loose, the discourse often shifts from "Oh god, there is a maniac on the loose", to "How do we protect ourselves? Let's learn from what the victims did wrong".

This seems proactive, but it tricks your brain into thinking that the victim deserved their fate because they were out at night, frequented the wrong part of town, or weren't alert enough. We want to believe we control our destiny by being more intelligent, better, blessed, or inherently lucky. Our empathy is replaced with sterile logic to try and make sense of things. A narcissist is capable of this in spades. Instead of protecting their sanity in a complicated world, they only watch their ego.

Lessons From Monsters 3
Mark David Chapman

A peek into the mind of a person that sees people as possessions is Mark David Chapman, the man who murdered John Lennon and part of the reason high schoolers everywhere have to read Catcher in the Rye (spoilers, it's fine). It should be stated that the doctors that have studied him after his arrest don't know what to make of a potential diagnosis. He had more problems than being entitled. It cannot be denied that his narcissism was like gasoline to a flame in the killer's mind.

Mark David Chapman grew up in a dysfunctional household with an abusive father and a doting mother (I told you this would be a pattern). His villain origin story (this is not conjecture; Chapman said this) was the wedgie he endured in elementary school. Realizing he was a nobody at school, he only had any power when protecting his mom from his dad's rages and in front of his "little people council". According to Chapman, this is the imaginary colony of tiny people that lived in the walls. These manifestations of Chapman's mental illness were his subjects in a fantasy world where he would act as their king. Like any powerful ruler, he would regularly engage in the mass murder of his people by stomping through their civilization like Godzilla. Despite the regular genocide, these people would worship Chapman and even offer him, counsel. It began the cycle of needing to be someone important that would doom both Chapman and John Lennon.

Between inflicting mass murder on his subjects, Chapman was a massive Beatles fan. Their earlier records were an undeniable comfort in what must have been a lonely life. Still, his least favorite was always John Lennon, and he would find any excuse to rant about him as he grew up. After the Beatles broke up, Chapman grew enraged with the former Beatle's antics. Chapman was set off by John Lennon's book *One Day at a Time*, which detailed his opulent post-Beatles life. The houses, yachts, and constant indulgence were infuriating for someone who sang about having no possessions. He thought of Lennon as an obnoxious, self-important hypocrite. While that assessment is not entirely wrong, Chapman felt betrayed by Lennon. There was an element of a childhood version of him feeling duped as he looked to the Beatles for comfort. These were his heroes, and the leader of that group owed it to his fans to remain the 16-year-old in a bowl cut and suit who sang about peace and love. He thought that Lennon had strayed too far from the ideals that made him love his music in the first place. He didn't know what he would do, but he knew that Lennon could not go on like this. Something had to be done.

Around this time, Chapman connected to JD Salinger's book *The Catcher in the Rye*. This is the coming-of-age story about Holden Caulfield, a teenager disillusioned with the level of phoniness that the adults around him subject him to. Holden sees himself as a rescuer (catcher) who saves children from falling to their deaths as they innocently play or, in this case, become cynical adults. Readers were only supposed to sympathize with Caulfield as he was a traumatized young man grappling with growing up and clearly could not handle change. It was a juvenile narcissistic perspective as Caufield thought he was the only one who could protect the innocence of youth. Kids like this should grow into adults who can roll through life's punches instead of wanting to freeze everything in place.

You can see the connection here with Lennon and wanting to save him from his phoniness. Chapman had the unfortunate habit of seeing everything around him as a sign justifying his twisted beliefs. Chapman did not only connect with Holden Caulfield; he wanted to be him so badly so he could finally be somebody. He resonated with the book's message so hard that he planned to shoot Lennon, and they would both disappear into the ink of the novel. It was a stupid plan, but Chapman was so convinced, his intentions were just that to him, nothing would go wrong.

Not even his little people council would co-sign the plan. You see, the bite-sized society had matured with Chapman and became a democracy that would cooperate with Chapman but had the agency to say no to him. All except one, The Child. He named his plan *Chapter 27* as, to him, it was a bonus chapter of *The Catcher in the Rye*, and he set out to "save" John Lennon.

Chapman set out alone in his quest to New York City to kill Lennon. Throughout his trip, he would come across things in his surroundings that he took as signs that the universe was giving his plan its blessings. Finally, he found himself in front of his childhood hero. The Child just whispered, "Do it, do it, do it," and Chapman shot Lennon five times as he attempted to flee. The severity of his situation only dawned on him when he did not, in fact, blend into the ink of *The Catcher in the Rye*, and police swiftly apprehended him.

Mark David Chapman pleaded guilty and got 25 to life in prison. This was against his legal counsel's advice, who thought they had a strong argument on an insanity plea. At the start, Mark blamed John Lennon, Satan, and everything except for himself. As the years wore on, he also claimed he wanted to shoot someone famous to gain notoriety but still fell short of expressing genuine remorse. To this day, he has been denied parole, and unless he can convince the board that he is a changed man who has learned from his mistakes and waited until Yoko Ono dies, he will stay in prison (Jack Jones, 2000).

Making Perfectionism Everyone Else's Problem

When we think of perfection, we often go back to the kid who cried in school over a B+, an anxious person that has internalized the unrealistic expectations they have been fed since birth. We see self-destructive behaviors and we sympathize with them. Scientists have found a link between perfectionist behaviors and narcissism. You would think that a narcissist experiencing this anxiety could be a source of doubt, and even humility when the smoke clears. However, that is not the case. These standards don't make them suffer; they are directed outward and can become a nightmare for others.

These are your micromanagers who pick on every aspect of a project or a process because it is not "perfect" or, in other words, not done their way. You see, the narcissist is the brain of the operation. The plan has to work; if it doesn't, everyone else doesn't understand their vision. A person confident in their team, abilities, and strategy would never need to micromanage so hard because they are busy leading the charge, clearing the path for everyone to have their best chance of success. A narcissist with no leadership abilities is incapable of this, but they can nitpick small details and dole out criticism.

Practicing Gratitude

The emotion of gratitude can be a powerful tool in healing. More and more practitioners are utilizing the feeling to make their patients feel physically and mentally better. This can be tricky for narcissists; gratitude can sometimes elude them. It might not even be downright malicious. Everyone has taken a loved one who went out of their way to do something nice for granted because we don't realize how much trouble it took. Gratitude requires you to enter someone else's shoes to discover how special it is that they chose to help you despite not gaining much from it. It's a part of the social contract we learn as children. Journaling about the things you are grateful for might feel a bit silly but remember you need to practice these behaviors so they can become part of your identity.

Consciously practicing gratitude has been shown to reduce stress, which can have a cascade effect on the body, including better heart health, immunity, and digestive issues. It forces you to pivot your normal state of cynicism and caution. While thinking grateful thoughts is a good start, it's not as effective as journaling them. A thought comes and goes like a breeze; you can't interact with or fully digest it but writing it down cements it in reality. Writing about sensitive topics can be a legitimate challenge, even if your next move includes burning the paper before anyone can read it. There is a catharsis to it, which is why so many teens gravitate to the practice to cope with their experiences (Emmons & Stern, 2013).

Try writing down what you are grateful for, how those things impact your life, and the other emotions around them. Once you get going, you might realize that you have more in this world than you think and owe much of it to others. You might even figure out other traits about yourself that can help you gain confidence (something that, paradoxically, a lot of narcissists lack). Here are some examples:

- I am thankful my parents let me live with them rent-free so I can save money and not be stressed about work.

- I am grateful for the physical health that allows me to move through the world easily.

- I am grateful I didn't give up on my progress at the gym, and I am now seeing results.

- I am thankful I have siblings I can lean on when things get rough.

- I am thankful that I have enough self-awareness to improve constantly.

Key Takeaways

- Narcissists feel entitled to materials and people, seeking validation through consumption and exaggeration.

- Narcissists engage in dehumanization of other people to justify their own bad behavior and view them as possessions.

- Fear of losing control or being at any disadvantage feeds insecurity.

- Narcissists constantly need attention and struggle with internal validation. It's a victory even if the attention is negative.

- Narcissists blame others for rejection or failure to preserve their ego.

- Narcissists can also struggle with perfectionism, and this can become a nightmare when this anxiety is projected outward.

- Practicing gratitude can be challenging for narcissists but has healing benefits such as reducing stress and fostering empathy.

- Journaling about gratitude helps solidify and appreciate the things and people in one's life.

HOW TO STOP NARCISSISTIC ENVY FROM DESTROYING YOUR RELATIONSHIPS

"Love doesn't die a natural death. Love has to be killed, either by neglect or narcissism."

- CRISS JAMI

Narcissists can suffer extreme envy or jealousy. No, those two terms are not interchangeable. Jealousy is an offensive emotion rooted in fear of loss. It is when you covet something being taken away from you, like an older sibling being jealous of a new baby because they feel they are taking away all their parent's attention. Envy is a defensive emotion based on inadequacy. It is coveting something that does not belong to us because we feel it would fill a void. You would experience this if your coworker got a promotion over you. It's not that you were replaced (that would be jealousy). You are staying static because you cannot measure up to your coworker. Regardless of the emotion, narcissists need to look over at another person's plate and this can be a catalyst that can destroy their relationships.

The Ugliness of Jealousy

Narcissists have an extreme fear of rejection, and rather than accepting that they can't control people or work on themselves to be a partner anyone would be thrilled to have, they externalize those fears. To put themselves at ease, selfish people will do whatever they can to make others see that their only path forward is with them. This often involves emotional and financial abuse, though it can escalate to physical abuse. The first step is to love bomb a person to get them to attach quickly. This means constant affection, gifts, and an uncharacteristically permissive and pleasant demeanor. The narcissist does all of this incredibly paradoxical behavior in the beginning because, one, they are being fueled by the high of a novel relationship, and two, because the other person, who is also in this whirlwind butterfly stage, needs to be able to have a tangible aspiration for when things go south. If there were good times, they could question whether or not they caused the change, not realizing that was the plan the whole time.

The next step is for the narcissist to throw their significant other off their axis through gaslighting. Gaslighting can have profound mental health consequences for those who experience it. We take our perceptions of reality for granted, but the second they don't align with someone else's who we trust and respect, we can go a bit nutty. This will put the person on edge, make them question everything, and see their narcissistic lover as their only point of contact for reality.

It also makes it so they disregard their feelings and memories, making them highly malleable. To maximize their influence, a narcissist will often isolate their significant other. They may get them to move in with them quickly and keep them away from their friends and family by manipulating them into thinking that they have bad friends or abusive parents. The significant other does not know that the people in their lives are kryptonite to narcissists because they can break the spell. Distance means that a family member can never see a personality change in the significant other or call out abusive behavior when they see it. Speaking of which, a narcissist will peel off the layers of self-esteem from their loved ones bit by bit.

At this point, the love bombing is over. Despite their insistence on loving someone, they will ensure that their SO will never see themselves as capable without being at the hip of the narcissist. A narcissist will make sure to let the SO know that no one else could ever find them attractive, that they are not smart enough to run the house on their own, and that they are lucky that the narcissist is so forgiving of their flaws and how they are getting more than they deserve all from the goodness of the narcissist's heart. You might be asking why people stay with people that treat them like garbage. Unfortunately, this happens all the time. Our brains can do some pretty irrational things when the respect of someone we love is on the line. All this ensures that a person is on a mental leash, chained to their narcissist without any agency.

Envy

Narcissists who see themselves as deserving of everything will envy those with the skills to take life by the horns. This is more seen in the people they cannot control, like colleagues and their children. A narcissistic parent can be seen as a person who is envious of their own child. Maybe it's their youth, innocence, or talent. These qualities that should be cherished can quickly become fuel for a narcissist. You have one of two possibilities. One is doubling down. This can be seen in insane stage parents like Joe Jackson.

He was a classic narcissist who took his frustrations with his middling music career on his children. He would force them to perform and, as their manager, made their lives hell as he tried to make a name for himself. It really came to a head when he realized how talented his son Michael was. This elementary-aged child had everything that Joe Jackson wanted, and he saw dollar signs and a legacy. He would beat his sons and force them to rehearse all night in pursuit of perfection. Even as an incredibly successful adult, Michael was still extremely afraid of his father, who mentally and physically tormented him.

This tiger parenting is born of one thing: to make a talented child a status symbol since narcissists cannot cultivate their own. They see it as a sacrifice that they make of time and money that they will hold over a child who never asked to be brought into this world or be the best at anything. As a result, the child will grow into an anxious adult who may have a warped perception of love and healthy relationships.

How Narcissism Limits Your Social Pool

The nature of narcissism severely limits the people you allow in your life, and often not for the better. Narcissists will pick people who, at best, drink the Kool-Aid of their awesomeness or, at worst, don't challenge them. We have already established that this locks you in arrested development, most likely in your teenage or young adult years, where you start making your own choices. However, this also limits your romantic prospects severely. You will never go after people that can offer you more than validation. It's not enough that you have a partner that can reassure you; it's that this person cannot outshine you in any way.

They cannot be more intelligent, sociable, or attractive because, to a narcissist, this reminds them of their inadequacy and a threat to the relationship. A clever or friendly person might see through their lies and figure out how insecure they are, and an attractive person will certainly leave for greater prospects. Once again, this is the fragility of the ego talking.

To keep that rejection from happening, narcissists will seek out people who are essentially the bare minimum in every aspect except their ability to feed their egos. Is that the foundation you want for a relationship with the person that may go on to parent your children? A person that you can just barely be able to stand? Why wouldn't you choose someone who can unleash your inner potential? A partner you can be proud to stand next to as an equal to face everything the world throws at you. Instead, narcissists purposely pick someone who may not be the best fit for this job, leading to inevitable resentment. Then when things start to fall apart, the narcissist can play the victim when in reality, through choices and shutting down their partner's self-esteem, they are in a mess of their own making.

Practice Compassion Instead of Envy

One of the biggest struggles for a narcissist is not only seeing yourself as a human but being okay with that. Your relationships struggle because you have absolutely no faith in yourself and instead of retreating inward, you lash out. You wouldn't feel the need to pull others into the abyss if you did not unconsciously feel that way about yourself.

When you feel emotional or make a mistake, it's okay to be disappointed, but see it as what it is: a part of the process and a lesson. It's when we screw up that we learn how to troubleshoot, be creative, and think outside of the box. There is no way to master anything if you don't know it inside out. That includes every conceivable way that things can go wrong.

By building up your own self-esteem, you will become a person who is capable of believing that people won't just leave them for no reason. And even if this does happen, it will hurt, but you know that the storm always passes. Hard times always suck, but coupling that with self-loathing can traumatize you and might create a cycle of over correction that will hurt other people. The worst part is, you will be blind to your behavior because you can justify claiming it defends your peace of mind.

Letting People Go

BoJack Horseman: Herb, I said I'm sorry.

Herb Kazzaz: Yeah, and I do not forgive you...No, I'm not going to give you closure. You don't get that...

BoJack Horseman: I really think that we'd both feel better if we–

Herb Kazzaz: ...I'm not gonna feel better. And I'm not gonna be your prop so you can feel better.

–Bojack Horseman

One of the hardest lessons for a narcissist is letting people go if they no longer want anything to do with you. This is the reality of how much control you have over other people. Even if you apologize and do a 180-degree turn on your demeanor and outlook, that person has every right to not validate that work by forgiving you. Part of your healing is realizing that the other person also has to heal, and part of that is never engaging with you again.

This can make you feel like all your progress is worthless, but that is just your persistent need for validation talking. Remember, you are not after a moral dessert; you improve yourself and do good in the world because that is ethical. By seeking out a person that does not want to hear from you, groveling, and trying to prove that you have changed, you only demonstrate that you still haven't weaned off the validation tap. You have once again busted into their life like the Kool-Aid man and demanded validation. If the person wants to contact you for closure, that is one thing, but if you try and guilt your way back into their good graces, you have a long way to go.

Key Takeaways

- Narcissists experience extreme envy and jealousy, with jealousy rooted in the fear of loss and envy stemming from feelings of inadequacy.

- Narcissists cope with their fears of rejection by seeking to control others through emotional and financial abuse.

- Narcissists often reel people in by using tactics like love bombing and gaslighting. They can work on making their significant other docile through isolation, emotional manipulation, verbal, and even physical abuse.

- Narcissistic parents may become envious of their own children's qualities and talents and may attempt to live vicariously through their kid.

- Letting go of people who no longer want to engage with a narcissist is a difficult but necessary lesson, as seeking validation and forcing contact only undermines personal growth and healing.

THE TRAP OF COMPLACENCY

"Some people think that the world revolves around them but even the Sun is not the center of the Universe."

- HALLE TEART

Everyone has something they aspire to; wealth, fame, love, and power are all things 99% of us must work to obtain. Narcissistic people are no different, except they often confuse magical thinking with results and become sorely disappointed if that identity is challenged. Ironically, narcissists will try every trick in the book to make people think they deserve praise except actually succeeding in praiseworthy things. They will either double down and insist they are a great person, or they will invent reasons why the heavens conspired against them. It's a vicious cycle of a lack of self-awareness and motivation that can lead to action.

Narcissists often go through a similar cycle that overthinkers do when getting something they want.

However, a lack of self-awareness can modify this cycle quite a bit. They see something novel that they want to accomplish. However, they are not motivated by increased confidence or tangible health or life improvement. If they can succeed, they can tell everyone how hard they have worked, be a source of inspiration and have something that puts them above the normies.

It's time to go full clip on this new thing; they buy books and equipment and, most importantly, tell everyone they know how their life will change. They start offering advice despite only starting a week ago. They direct every conversation to this, making it the center of their identity.

Then something happens, and things start getting a little challenging. Instead of powering through, a narcissist will begin to compromise because any form of discomfort goes against their programming. Still, they hang on to their new shiny identity by playing dumb, compromising, and assuring everyone that they are still hard at work. The people in their lives start to notice these slip-ups if they become apparent. If the narcissist is on a weight loss journey, this can look like a social media post showing off fast food instead of that fresh food they insisted was delicious. At some point, someone may inquire what the deal is. The narcissist goes on high alert, lest they be unmasked like a Scooby-Doo villain. They start to sidestep, make excuses, justify, and lie about their progress. They may also go radio silent about the subject, hoping they can make up for the lost progress before anyone notices. Inevitably, people catch on, and then the hackles go up. More and more people see the narcissist in a less-than-ideal position, and they cannot have that. They reach the final stage and quit, but this isn't the type of failure where someone does self-reflection and takes lessons from the experience. No, this is quitting while taking no accountability. They will blame anything and everyone. Their job made them too tired to put the work in; their family distracted them; they used the wrong book or programs, etc. Narcissists will do anything to depersonalize their failures because that is the only way to keep their egos intact.

Many narcissists ride that fuel of novelty but quickly burn out at the follow-through stage. They expect things to work out because they are unique or spend so much money. If you read my previous book on overthinking, you know that this is the addictive, easy part, and a narcissist will look like Sideshow Bob stepping on dozens of rakes while they repeatedly fall into this trap. Sometimes they get it in their head that becoming a source of inspiration is impossible with that mindset, but there is a third option between success and failure.

The Safety Of The Victim

While success is greeted by the admiration of others, there is another energy a narcissist can adopt as fuel, and that is sympathy. While not as satisfying as adulation and validation, especially for an overt narcissist, it can fill the covert narcissist's cup without all the pesky work. Once the narcissist enters this mindset, they can become trapped in it. Suddenly, the rules don't apply to them as they go through life. It's not their fault they can't succeed; the world was against them from the start. They no longer need to have any agency and become comfortable with the universe pulling them by their nose. If things go wrong, that is more fuel for their victim complex. They have someone else to blame for their misfortune, which is excellent because now self-improvement is out of their control.

Taking on this identity can seriously blow their ego, and they start lashing out. Their misbehavior is blamed on poor mental health, frustration, and the person on the receiving end who just happened to push the wrong button that day. We have all snapped at someone for these reasons, but the difference between a less-than-stellar human moment and a pattern of narcissistic behavior comes down to what someone does next. If they apologize for being short, take responsibility, and try not to lose their temper again, then all can be forgiven. However, a narcissist will double down, give an "I'm sorry you felt that way" apology, or just continue the behavior.

Eventually, the recipient of all their frustrations gets wise and stops putting up with the excuses. At this point, instead of doing some self-reflection, it is easier to just find a new person to garner sympathy from. This mindset is so dangerous because soon, narcissists will start believing in their own lies, and now they have to maintain that as part of their identity. They will even resort to victimizing themselves just to keep the tap of sympathy from drying up. This is where compliment fishing comes in.

- *Narcissist: God, my hair is a mess today (it looks the same as it always does).*

  Friend: Please, your hair looks great!

- *Narcissist: I'm so stupid.*

  Friend: That's not true!

- *Narcissist: Everyone hates me (is speaking to a friend).*

  Friend: I think you are pretty great!

It's about controlling the narrative. The recipient is given no choice but to supply validation. When your friend is feeling down, you want to cheer them up. Narcissists use this compulsion to make people validation factories. By making any person perceive flaws front and center, the narcissist will never be surprised by the other person catching on to it and forming their own opinion because the narcissist has already made it for them. It may be a negative quality, but it's the control that matters.

You Are Invited to a Grandiose Pity Party

Terminal uniqueness describes the mindset in which an individual believes that their specific circumstances exempt them from the rules that everyone else has to go by. You see this a lot when a narcissist has to make an excuse. Their diet failed not because they didn't watch what they ate, it's because their metabolism is so slow that they can drink water and gain weight. They don't need to work on lashing out, their childhood trauma makes criticism a trigger for them. Every misfortune in their life isn't a culmination of bad choices, they are just things that happen to them like a storm swept in.

The Ambition Of
Hollywood Leading Men

It's an age-old tale of individuals venturing to Hollywood not only in pursuit of a career but also to leave behind a lasting legacy. Over the years, countless actors have tried their luck in the movie industry, each with unique backgrounds and philosophies on how to rise to the top. Despite his undeniable success, Dwayne Johnson, also known as "The Rock," serves as a cautionary example. Hailing from humble beginnings, Johnson used his athletic physique and magnetic charisma to make a name for himself in wrestling. He possessed it all: a massive fanbase, a distinct identity to capitalize on, influence in the industry, and multiple championship titles. However, he understood that more than technical ability would be needed to guarantee him a spot at the pinnacle.

The Rock had his sights set on Hollywood and was determined to make it there, no matter the obstacles. Yet, his path to becoming a household name was far from easy. While he found some success with films like *The Scorpion King*, he also experienced setbacks with less well-received movies such as *The Tooth Fairy*. Nonetheless, a figure like Dwayne Johnson couldn't admit defeat. At some point, he realized that merely being an actor wouldn't suffice—he had to transform himself into a brand, packaged and sold to the industry. This approach eventually paid off, leading him to star in high-budget franchises and become the highest-paid actor in Hollywood.

However, becoming Dwayne Johnson™ changed the star, not necessarily for the better. As a brand, he had an image to protect. Consequently, he took on roles featuring Dwayne Johnson engaging in typical action-hero antics. He became typecast, playing the same character in every film: a tough yet slightly goofy strongman who leads his group to victory. By confining himself to this box, he sacrificed the authenticity that quality moviegoers appreciate, even in big-budget popcorn flicks. Audiences want to see characters who feel human, not demigods. Consequently, his roles often lacked tension, as viewers knew he would never lose a fight, or the scripts became convoluted, attempting to inject stakes while adhering to contractual obligations.

Another critical blow to Dwayne Johnson's career was his preoccupation with maintaining his image and ensuring his roles portrayed him in the best light possible. As a result, he failed to forge lasting connections with talented directors and should have improved his acting skills. With the rise of wrestlers turned actors like Dave Bautista and John Cena, it is evident that wrestlers no longer have limited range. Multiple paths can be pursued to shape a legacy.

Both Bautista and Cena possess different skill sets and personality traits, with Cena echoing Dwayne Johnson's approach. Bautista, known as a powerhouse in the wrestling ring, lacked witty one-liners or charm. Instead, he was an intimidating force, a tank. On the other hand, John Cena followed Dwayne's model in his wrestling career. His character remained consistent, never truly becoming a villain because he understood the importance of his image to his young fans. While this predictability drew the ire of adult wrestling fans, the children regarded him as a hero. Cena went to great lengths to brand himself as kid-friendly, even setting records for the most Make-A-Wish visits by any celebrity. Bautista and Cena faced a choice to break free from the WWE's grasp: follow the Rock's path and become more brand than man or dare to explore something new.

Bautista's acting career turned into a Cinderella story. Many doubted the muscle-bound behemoth could portray a character beyond the dim-witted henchman. However, Bautista approached his new endeavor with utmost seriousness, undergoing training and reaching out to esteemed directors, making it clear he was open to their vision. James Gunn, set to direct Marvel Studios' *Guardians of the Galaxy*, recognized Bautista's potential and cast him as Drax, a role that may have seemed typecast at first glance. Yet, when audiences witnessed the movie, they were blown away by Bautista, who often stole the show from A-listers like Chris Pratt and Zoe Saldana. In the role of Drax, Bautista embodied a tough man grappling with the loss of his family. He delivered a consistent and captivating performance, showcasing his comedic timing, dramatic range, and excellent timing. He continued to prove his acting prowess in subsequent projects, such as *Blade Runner*. Bautista understood he couldn't rely on his previous success or attempt to control a studio's vision. Instead, he humbly dedicated himself to honing his craft, working with the industry, and, most importantly, taking risks.

John Cena, too, represents what Dwayne Johnson's career could have been had he not hindered himself. Cena has put significant effort into his acting career, accepting roles in comedies and romcoms. He has become a linchpin in the DC Cinematic Universe, not by seeking the limelight, but by enhancing the projects he is involved in. His standout role as Peacemaker showcased his natural comedic timing and surprising emotional depth. Cena was willing to openly display vulnerability, sob on screen, lose fights, be talked down to by other characters, and share the spotlight. Meanwhile, Dwayne Johnson finds his career at a critical juncture, with his self-imposed obstacles starting to catch up with him. His highly anticipated project, *Black Adam*, was meant to symbolize his ascension as DC's biggest asset. However, his ego took over and exerted too much control over the project. Public interest in *Black Adam*, especially as a standalone film, was limited, particularly among casual moviegoers who aren't avid comic fans. To create an entry point for audiences, it would have been wise to involve Black Adam's nemesis, Shazam, who already had a well-received film. Yet, Dwayne prioritized being the center of the story, resulting in the removal of Shazam from the film. Instead, he pushed for Superman's inclusion, teasing an ultimate showdown with little sense and little demand. Unfortunately, *Black Adam* lacked compelling storytelling, emotional depth, vulnerability, tension, and a well-rounded personality. The contractual obligations and Dwayne's micromanagement ultimately sank the project, as he solely viewed it as a vehicle for his own stardom, failing to see the bigger picture. This misstep impacted the DC franchise, affecting writers and other actors, and tarnished Dwayne Johnson's career. He is no longer the guaranteed box office draw he once was. He must learn from this experience to reclaim his legacy and pivot toward more serious acting roles or risk robbing himself of a meaningful and lasting impact.

Not Everyone Sees Things from Just Your Perspective

To someone who has not learned empathy, this is an attractive argument. Instead of making a compelling argument, a narcissist uses emotions against the other person to win an argument. On the surface, this is a legitimate argument. However, you are forgetting that the thing you are arguing about doesn't exist in a vacuum, and people with different perspectives will have different experiences. Let's say you have a side hustle as a clown for children's parties. You have a costume and makeup and can make balloon animals so intricate that even adults line up for them. Now you are invited to your nephew's birthday party as a guest and agree to go on your precious day off. When you arrive, your in-law is vexed that you are in standard family picnic attire, sans large shoes, a red nose, and balloons. Being blindsided has also caused your emotions to go up a few notches. Your in-law does not understand why this is such a big deal. It all makes sense.

- You are family.

- You have the experience and the stuff to give the kids a great time.

- It would mean a lot to the nephew.

- They can save money.

- You are there anyway, and it would only be for an hour.

- Did they mention you are family?

There is only an argument if you remove all emotions and look at it from the in-law's perspective. By being obnoxiously pedantic, the in-laws fail to see that you agreed to go to the party to spend time with family while sipping on alcohol and gossiping. When you have a day off, you expect not to have to wrangle kids and make sure your smile is painted straight.

Why This is Keeping You from Becoming Great

Lex Luthor: Give it back. I saw everything. I saw how to save the world. I could have made everyone see. If it wasn't for you, I could have saved the world.

Superman: If it had mattered to you, Luthor, you could have saved the world years ago.

-All Star Superman

Only relying on yourself is a surefire way to never get anywhere. Humanity only survived because we built communities, created families, and pooled resources to create something bigger than nature could imagine. And yet, narcissists regularly shirk this gift in favor of doing everything on their own.

Failing to See the Big Picture

If you take any lesson from the media that features narcissistic characters that do not change, it's this: they always lose because they refuse to account for the wills of others. Narcissists can become delusional about their place in other people's stories and vastly overestimate their influence on others. They become complacent because the circle they have chosen to surround themself with guarantees they will never be challenged or come face to face with their own shortcomings. That is, until someone does something unexpected.

Instead of working with people to see how they tick, looking at their motivations, and learning from their struggles, narcissists will disregard their perspectives entirely. As a result, plans become rigid, and banks of people are doing exactly what you expect. However, people have the annoying ability to do unexpected things when the chips are down. An excellent example of this would be the Russian invasion of Ukraine. Vladimir Putin thought his army could march in, take the country, and be home in time for dinner. Any world leader trapped between an army and a panicked populace would run away to safety in another country and watch as their country is plundered. When news broke of the impending invasion, the mood was outrage tinged with a reservation that Putin would get what he wanted. But when everyone checked in the next day, something amazing happened. Zelensky surprised everyone.

President Zelensky, a former comedian who played a president on television, was no one's idea of a great leader. His presidency had been pretty unremarkable up until that point. Still, he became the closest thing to the president from the movie *Independence Day* that the world stage had ever seen. The Ukrainian populace was emboldened seeing their leader refusing to leave the front lines, demanding ammunition instead of a flight out. Patriotism soared in the country, and the masses decided to fight until the bitter end. It was easy for the whole world to support someone with so much love and inspiring bravery. As a result, this invasion, which was supposed to be an easy win for Russia, has unraveled into an unmitigated disaster.

Since the Russian army had to prove their meddling with an opponent more formidable than frightened elderly and families, they were exposed for being disorganized. The might of the Russian military complex that brought the world to its knees during the Cold War has become a bit of a laughingstock. Putin was so confident in his invasion that he went all in, and now there is no ending to this where he doesn't lose face. It is a narcissist's worst nightmare, and he is living it.

Stale Vision

You don't need to be in a giant military conflict to see how your tunnel vision can affect the outcome of your life's work. Despite what you may think, you are not an expert on everything and will probably need advice and emotional support at some point. Narcissists tend to want as few fingers in as few pies as possible and sometimes none at all. Issues quickly arise when the project gets out of hand that are obvious to everyone except the narcissist.

- **Compromise**: Some aspects will fall by the wayside as the narcissist is pulled in several directions. This often interests the narcissist the least, such as logistics.

- **Unstable work environment**: As there is no delegation present and a narcissist is either too busy or is making assumptions about the effectiveness of how they communicated their plan, tensions will rise on site. Workers will feel unappreciated and will not be motivated to do their best or develop creative solutions.

- **No feedback**: If the narcissist has unilateral control of the project, people might be less willing to give honest feedback on the work environment and the project outcome. No one wants to be the bearer of bad news, and small issues can turn into full-blown fires quickly. When things do go wrong, the narcissist will be blindsided, leading to...

- **The shattering illusion**: If the narcissist had any sort of good reputation, it would go up in smoke as the stress of the project, combined with a mediocre or lousy product, will make people wonder why they ever trusted this person. People will be reluctant to work with you, and your body of work will no longer be attractive to prospective collaborators.

It's Never Too Late to Learn Empathy

For a narcissist seeking healing and personal growth, Kant's Categorical Imperative theory can essentially be a cheat sheet on how to treat others. Kant surmised the principle of acting in a way that should be universally applied to all individuals. This means that people should consider the moral implications and consequences and act accordingly in how they would like to be treated, rather than a mere means to their own ends.

Embracing the Categorical Imperative can be transformative for a narcissist who looks out for number one and feeds off external validation and admiration. It encourages a shift in perspective from self-centeredness to empathy and respect for the autonomy and dignity of others. A narcissist can start to recognize the harmful effects of their self-centered behavior and develop a genuine concern for the well-being of others because they can take a step back and reflect on their decision (Johnson & Cureton, 2022).

Learning to Take Responsibility

Repairing Bridges

To mend a broken bridge, taking responsibility is the first step. It's not enough to say sorry, though, and you have to avoid the pitfalls of bad apologies, which can look like:

- *I'm sorry you felt that way.*

- *It was just a joke.*

- *I shouldn't have trusted xyz.*

- *You probably want me to die.*

- *This is really hard for me right now.*

- *I have suffered so much because of this.*

There is a decent rubric to an apology that gets at the root of what the other person needs to hear and believe, not what is easier to get through with your pride intact.

- **Take responsibility:** Say what you did and the observable effects. Do not blame or try to explain your actions.

- **Be empathetic:** Show the person you understand what they felt and recognize the validity of those emotions, no matter how unpleasant.

- **Show your sincerity:** Put as little distance as possible between you, calling or talking in person, and not texting or emailing your apology. Do not attempt to bribe a person for their forgiveness and avoid flowery language you would never use in any other situation.

- **Be specific:** If you dropped off the map and worried your family, apologize for being so careless and stressing everyone out, not that you were not around to sign for your sister's Amazon packages. Being vague or shifting the offending action reads as trying to skirt responsibility.

- **Make amends:** Try to make the other person complete again if they allow it. If you broke something, replace it. If you started a rumor, do your best to fess up to people instead of letting it continue to run wild.

- **Listen to the other person:** This one may hurt, but you must take in what the other person says. They may correct you on their feelings or may not be ready to accept the apology. Repeat it back to them so they know that you understand. Accept it with grace and honor their wishes regardless of what they say. They may not accept the apology, as is their prerogative.

- **Reflect:** Regardless of the outcome, sit with your emotions or, even better, write them down. Even if the result isn't what you hoped, you got your feelings off your chest and cleared the air, so at least everyone knows where they stand. That takes courage, and you should feel proud you made yourself vulnerable. Write what you have learned and how you will continue to apply these lessons in your daily life.

Michael: [scoffs] Oh. Oh, okay. Ah, I get it, I get it. You want me to admit that I was wrong. You want me to say, "Oh, Chidi, I'm so sorry. Because I didn't understand human ethics, and you do, it made me feel insecure, and I lashed out. And, oh, please help me because I feel so, so lost and vulnerable."

Chidi Anagonye: Yes.

Michael repeats the exact same apology but in a more heartfelt tone

—The Good Place

Key Takeaways

- Narcissists often confuse magical thinking with real effort, setting themselves up for disappointment.

- Narcissists go through a cycle of pursuing something they want, but since their motivation is driven by external validation rather than personal growth, they run out of gas.

- Narcissists may engage in self-sabotage and compromise when faced with challenges, while maintaining the appearance of progress to others.

- Narcissists tend to blame external factors and avoid taking accountability for their failures, protecting their ego, and depersonalizing their shortcomings.

- Complacency can limit a narcissist's potential and prevents them from seeing the bigger picture.

- Relying solely on oneself and lacking empathy for others can lead to stagnation and missed opportunities for personal and professional development.

- Learning empathy, taking responsibility, and offering sincere apologies are crucial steps for narcissists to repair relationships.

FROM SELF-LUST TO SELF-LOVE

"Narcissus weeps to find that his Image does not return his love."

- MASON COOLEY

The journey to self-love can be an arduous one. A typical person may seek it through therapy, enriching hobbies, and cultivating friendships. A narcissist, on the other hand, stands in a bit of a paradox. On the surface, they love themselves—that's like their thing. However, their grandiosity, paranoia, and lack of self-awareness can lead them to baffling choices in expressing that self-love. It leads to the classic divide between narcissists and those who radiate confidence. A confident person will pursue challenges they know they can handle, whether they succeed or not, and knows that they will stand out when they have earned that right. A narcissist, on the other hand, might pick the easier route and focus on aesthetics. This can have profound reverberations on how they are perceived and the people they surround themselves with. Let's just say there is a chasm between what the public sees on the outside looking in and what the narcissist thinks they see.

Buying Admiration

Riley: This will be a real chain! Oh yeah, I can't wait for people to start hatin' on me! I can't wait!

Huey: So, you judge your success based on the amount of ill-will you generate from those around you?

—The Boondocks

One of the easiest ways to gain status is to swipe your credit card enough times. Society judges us on several things, first and foremost with our ability to consume. Clothes, shoes, jewelry, and property are all ways to fill our cup in an attempt to think we are building meaningful status. There is nothing wrong with cultivating a personal aesthetic and buying things with the money you earn. It's one of the few joys we have on this planet. However, there has to be something underneath all those expensive clothes. If not, you are literally just an empty suit.

It goes without saying that trying to buy self-respect is a quick way to frustration and severe credit card debt. Unfortunately, it's a trap that narcissists fall into again and again. Researchers posit that they seek a few things when they not only consume, but do so loudly:

- It's an easy way to stand out and look unique.

- By standing out, they hope that someone they are attracted to takes notice and pursues them.

- Buying something can make it seem like your life has meaning and is making progress, and you want to prove that to yourself and everyone around you.

- It fills your self-imposed sense of materialism, which you believe everyone else around you values the same way. You are nothing without a tight fit and a house full of possessions.

Essentially, narcissists have confused the ability to spend money with worth (Sedikides & Hart, 2022). If you do not cultivate other aspects of your life, your self-esteem will crash harder than your credit score.

How Narcissists Look to Everyone Else

Signature Look of Superiority

—Star Wars: Revenge of the Sith: The Visual Dictionary, Entry on Count Dooku

When someone thinks about narcissism, they often go for appearance first. While narcissists don't wear a uniform, they will let their appearance dictate how they want the world to see them, which is a person of higher social standing for the most part. This includes brand named clothes, expensive blinding jewelry, heavy makeup, and showing off more skin. This does not mean every woman in a crop top or man in a muscle tee is a secret narcissist. However, if you look at the whole picture, it becomes obvious. People are pretty good at picking a narcissist from a lineup. If a person in a Gucci belt is nothing but sweet, the beholder might chalk it up to poor fashion taste. However, if the owner of that same Gucci belt starts to get short with a waiter, there will be no more room for nuance, and they will be clocked as narcissists.

Body Language

Despite their best efforts to hide it, narcissists can be easily spotted by how they carry themselves. Just because you don't have your nose in the air doesn't mean you aren't constantly telegraphing signs. Humans are very good at spotting someone who is disingenuous, which, unfortunately, is common in NPD. Remember, this population may not have been exposed to healthy human emotions or connections. They can try to fake it with eye contact or a smile, but if they don't quite grasp the subtleties, their eyes can read as cold or too intense. The smile can either be oddly closed or show too many teeth. Smiling is a universal gesture in all humans, and there is a social context to using one. If narcissists aren't quite keen on generating them naturally, they will look like they learned to smile by reading instructions.

Then there is their posture. Narcissists with little self-assurance will tend to overcompensate in their stance.

Their posture is often stiff as opposed to the ease a person with actual confidence typically has. Once again, these are not hard rules, but can be combined with how narcissists carry themselves in public. A narcissist may try to overwhelm the space they are in by moving up close or trying to tower over a person if they are tall. If you have ever seen two meatheads argue at a bar, you see this in full display. Suddenly, their chests puff up, and their shoulders are so squared back it's a wonder they don't dislocate. They then try to get their opponent to step back by ramming their pecs into each other. It's all about dominating the space (*Body Language – Narcissism and How to Survive It*, 2018).

Narcissists must also gauge how they respond to their environment; even a micro expression can ring an alarm bell. Any number of innocuous behaviors can make people uneasy. One big tell is a mismatch between the surrounding emotions and a narcissist's (lack of) reaction. Investigators often use these observations to catch criminals who have no idea how to reconcile their guilty actions with innocence. For example, some people with narcissistic traits may seem eerily calm while the world is crashing around them. Internet sleuths immediately noticed this phenomenon in the body cam footage of Brian Laundrie and Gabby Petitio. In the footage, Gabby was hysterical and clearly in crisis. Meanwhile, Brian smiled and charmed the cops (Britta Zeltmann, 2023). Even if you have done nothing wrong, seeing your significant other sobbing and panicking should kick up your adrenaline just a little.

A narcissist might find themselves talking loudly and overpowering a conversation. While other neurodivergent conditions can cause this if you also go through an entire 20-minute conversation without coming up for air, it's worth ensuring your counterpart is not annoyed or overwhelmed. Narcissists may also be a bit more handsy. Without realizing it, a narcissist can violate another person's personal space and boundaries with a simple hold of the shoulder or waist. When you don't rely on empathy, your brain might ask why anyone would have an issue being touched by you. After all, you mean no harm, you washed your hands, and you want to be friendly.

Touch, however, to some people, can be an extremely vulnerable affair, and out of fear of retaliation they may not even tell you that they have this boundary in place. A good rule of thumb is to give people their space, especially if you can see through their body language that this is important to them. Things to look out for are if they stop engaging in a conversation, step back when you step forward, or move away from touch. While rejection can hurt when you put yourself out there, if you react emotionally to it, everyone in the vicinity will want nothing to do with you.

So, what do you do? For now, practice makes perfect, and you will need examples to work on. Luckily the best model is the person right in front of you. We have covered this before, but modeling matches your body language with the person you speak to. It is a cheat sheet to subtle human interaction. If the person you are talking to is at ease, match that energy. You don't need to try and overpower every interaction. If that is your tact, it will blow up in your face when everyone sees you as exhausting to be around since they tire themselves unconsciously by mirroring your bravado. You should also treat conversations like a game of catch, letting each person maintain half of the interaction. You can learn a lot from engaging with other people. Stop and listen to what they have to say. Don't formulate a response or try to redirect a conversation to a topic you are more familiar with. Sit down and learn from others to be more well-rounded rather than relying on yourself.

The Emperor Has No Clothes

What a narcissist fails to realize is that if you want to form a connection with a person that can give you validation, it takes more than flashy clothes to get the job done. Most people do not care about buying designer brands and having a nice car if that is all you can offer. As we learned with Elliot Rogers, a rich kid who could have had a perfectly normal, if not entitled, life had he known how to interact with others, you quickly become an empty suit if you have nothing else to offer. Look at the media that stars narcissists. If they are central to the story, they need something else that justifies why people keep them around.

Tony Stark is a genius millionaire playboy philanthropist even before the suit. Sherlock from the BBC show can be insufferable. Still, he brilliantly solves mysteries (and being played by Benedict Cumberbatch didn't hurt) using his powers of deduction and showed he was willing to open himself up to his best friend, John Watson. This isn't just for the purposes of the story; an audience needs to like a person who, by all accounts, is totally obnoxious so they don't turn off their TVs in frustration.

The real world is a lot more complicated. Narcissists might be unable to grow, challenge themselves, and shape themselves into someone who might have something to offer. Instead, they think that flashing a watch or taking advice from a pickup artist is a substitute for real human connection. Material possessions will only get you so far with people who value those things, and they will probably use your limited skillset to their advantage.

In the end, all you are left with is battered self-esteem, since, in your eyes, you should be rolling in potential partners. You have all the trappings of a provider, but no one is biting. This will inevitably lead to lashing out. Or you will reject everyone by putting up defense mechanisms such as:

- Everyone only goes after jerks! I'm right here!

- All men/women are the same!

- They are just after my looks/money/status!

- I bought them dinner, and they didn't go home with me; what a gold digger!

When your pride has been wounded, the ego slips into that victim mentality.

Wearing An Obvious Costume

She's brought a ludicrously capacious bag, what's even in there, huh? Flat shoes for the subway or lunch pail? I mean, Greg, it's monstrous. It's gargantuan. You could take it camping. You could slide it across the floor after a bank job.

—Tom, Succession

No one is more attuned to peasants trying to enter the clubhouse than high society types. A narcissist's dream is to enter an elite world where they can influence the mere mortals of the middle and lower classes. They have spent their entire lives looking up to the wealthy and coveting their fashion, cars, and powerful lifestyles. Since entering these spaces is next to impossible, some settle for attempting to dress the part of being wealthy. There is a difference between clothes being expensive and looking expensive.

There is an adage: money talks, and wealth whispers. You can get an entertaining lesson in this by watching the show *Succession*. The wardrobe direction is authentic in the way old money presents itself. They would most likely be wearing something that doesn't quite stand out but is worth more than we make in a month. Their clothes are often timeless and well-fitting and are either taken care of by staff or rotated out frequently. The brands they wear focus more on their overall aesthetic rather than splashing their name everywhere. There is cohesion and ease to everything that looks expensive and quiet. That's because they don't need to announce their wealth to everyone; they can look at their bank app, realize they are rich beyond measure, and remember they don't have to care what anyone thinks.

People that try to fit into these clubs often come off as desperate and gullible rather than wealthy. Even if they have a decent balance in their checking account, they often parade around in what they think rich people wear instead of studying fashion. They fall for ads that are targeted at people who want to be wealthy. Their products are priced at a point that can hurt your credit score but are just attainable enough, so buying them can be seen as an accomplishment and a status symbol (Jill Krasny, 2014).

How Your Narcissism Can Make You a Mark

Narcissism can be a metaphor for a biological phenomenon called the *Handicapped Principal*. Think of a peacock. Male peacocks have a bright train of feathers designed to be heavy and conspicuous to attract mates. It seems like a simple principle; female birds are impressed with the bold colors and displays of plumage and decide they want to get it on with this impressive male specimen. But it makes less sense when you look at the display in the context of the rest of the environment. The feathers are heavy, making it impossible for the bird to hide and make for a convenient place for a predator to grip. This is where this principle comes into play. A peacock could have only so many feathers before nature started to correct its course. Birds that survived until mating season looked nice and proved to females that they were biologically fit to handle all those feathers and survive. Birds that had more to offer than the longest feathers attracted females and got to get their freak on.

This is highly reminiscent of the human experience. While peacocks have feathers, men have their own ways of attracting women. Muscles, an attractive face, and conspicuous consumption are all plumage for men–or so they think. For most healthy relationships, this only goes so far. Most people need something more profound to maintain the relationship beyond the initial butterfly stage. But some narcissists press on, showing off their cars on social media, flashing money on their Tinder profiles, and basically telling (or exaggerating) anyone who would listen how much capital they make (Sedikides & Hart, 2022).

It comes as no surprise that there has been a societal backlash to this behavior. Men with sports cars or trucks are mocked for attempting to compensate for something.

Their lack of confidence is so bare for the world to see that it can make them a target. A person who wears their lack of confidence like a neon sign can signal everything a manipulator needs to know:

- The narcissist is easily swayed by flattery.

- They have disposable income.

- They like to show off.

- They may crave affection and companionship.

- They have little self-awareness when it comes to their naivety.

- The narcissist can become dependent on the manipulator and will do anything to turn on that tap of external validation.

Just like that, you are a potential target for people who see you as a means to an end rather than a person. You don't even need to be a wallet with a heartbeat. If you have any sort of power or influence or can provide a service, a manipulator will ring you dry, and you won't even realize it. All someone needs to do is let you believe you have control when they are pulling the strings. It does not help that narcissists tend to be hypersensitive to fear. They will make snap decisions if they fear something negative is on the horizon to control the situation. Anyone savvy enough to manipulate a narcissist can use this to their advantage (Ronningstam & Baskin-Sommers, 2013).

The Armor of Self-Esteem

Now, you might be saying, isn't inflated self-esteem the problem in narcissism? While it is one way of framing the problem, the root issue is a lack of belief in oneself. You will do anything to prop up this image of yourself rather than foster and have faith in what is already there. We are not talking about material possessions or positions of power, all things that can disappear instantly. It's about believing you are capable without cheerleaders or material objects.

A person with self-respect would never need to show people how well-adjusted they think they are. They prove it to themselves every day by taking care of their bodies and finances and constantly developing new skills. Self-respect leads ironically to treating others with respect as you never feel like you are in competition or see the world in ways people can benefit or hurt you. You see others as fully realized humans, which will no longer scare you. Partners are more than sexual vending machines; customers are more than just a credit card number; kids are more than a chance to relive your lost childhood. You lose the blinders of how people fit into your world and start to see how you do into their world (Kristin Neff, 2011).

A person who respects themselves and others will soon begin to learn from their peers and their environment without the fear of failure hanging over their head. They will happily go to experts in the field because being in the presence of someone with the advantage of intelligence no longer makes them feel small or insignificant. New emotions, such as reverence or excitement, can creep in.

If you are secure in yourself, even people trying to knock you down can never get one over on you. Why? Because you have faith in your resilience and self-image. A stranger questioning your masculinity or femininity will sound like white noise because they can no longer shatter your ego.

Get Comfortable With Being Uncomfortable

One thing you can do to foster self-respect is to get out of your comfort zone. Go learn a new skill entirely out of your wheelhouse. If you think you can handle it, take a class where you can come face-to-face with fellow beginners and people who outclass you. The first thing you make will be bad, and you must sit with that. It's never a good feeling not to measure up. The actual test of character is not nailing your oil painting or ceramic pot on the first try; it's screwing up, learning, and returning for more. Think about all the adjectives you would use to describe a person like this. Words like resilient, confident, determined, eager, and adaptable come to mind. Over time, you will feel genuine pride over your progress as you remember all the attempts it took to get there. That is way more satisfying than getting something you decided you were entitled to. You put tangible effort in, and it's paying off. A hint you received in class may have paid off, and you have just practiced taking advice from someone else instead of just winging your process.

Key Takeaways

- Narcissists ironically struggle with genuine self-love due to their lack of self-awareness, fragile identity, and paranoia.

- Narcissists may try to buy admiration through material possessions, but this approach is doomed for being shallow and unsustainable.

- Narcissists can be easily identified by their appearance, including flashy clothing, expensive jewelry, and heavy makeup.

- Body language can betray narcissism, helping people key into traits such as cold eye contact, forced smiles, and domineering postures.

- Some narcissists attempt to dress and act like wealthy individuals to gain acceptance, but their desperation and lack of understanding make them easy targets for manipulation.

- Building genuine self-esteem and self-respect is essential for overcoming narcissism, which involves believing in oneself, having the humility to learn from others, and stepping out of your comfort zone.

CURTAILING THE
WRATH OF NARCISSISM

"The 'I' is the ego that we must avoid at any cost, if we truly wish to be different from narcissists. Instead of using 'I' repeatedly, it would be wise to replace it with 'we'."

- MWANANDEKE KINDEMBO

Picture this familiar scene. You are at a congested intersection, and the light has just turned yellow. To some people, this means to slow down, but to others, it just means "Speed up; I have places to be." A person goes through the now clearly red light and then realizes they are now stuck in the middle of the intersection. They fly in a rage and honk at all the cars in front of them to speed it up, even though it's impossible. This driver is lashing out at other drivers because he looks stupid, blocking the intersection. That is a taste of the wrath narcissism brings; it is irrational and not only destructive to everyone around you but will poison you as well.

Emotional Dysregulation

Rocket: You don't know anything about me, loser.

Yondu: I know everything about you. I know you play like you're the meanest and the hardest but actually you're the most scared of all.

Rocket: Shut up!

Yondu: I know you... push away anyone who's willing to put up with you 'cause just a little bit of love reminds you of how big and empty that hole inside you actually is...I know who you are, boy. Because you're me!

–Guardians of the Galaxy Volume 2

Narcissists can suffer from extreme emotional dysregulation. You might be carrying a lot of regret regarding how you have unleashed your insecurities on others. You have to work on forgiving yourself before you can solve this. Remember, forgiveness does not mean that you start looking for excuses or justifying your behaviors. It means that you realize what is done is done and that your actions have led to the direct suffering of someone else and recognize that you need to change because you want to be better. If you decide to throw a pity party or punish yourself, that is not the same thing as progress, especially if you go out of your way to tell people about it. The only way you can begin to make things right is to be better. Not for some moral dessert or to get someone back into your life, but because you want to be someone who puts some good into the world.

Why do Narcissists Get So Angry?

As we have discussed before, anger is a secondary emotion. It burns so hot that it often overpowers a more profound feeling. For you, it might be shame, weakness, or fear of rejection. Realizing that you are that vulnerable is a bitter pill to swallow, especially to a group of people that like to be in control. Instead, those complicated emotions are packaged into anger because that emotion is more manageable for our egos to deal with. Those other emotions are often directed inward, but anger shoots out. When you turn up the heat in exchange, the other person is liable to start lashing out as well, which can become a justification for their being irrational. See if any of these tactics are familiar to you during a confrontation:

- Turning even minor criticism into full-blown character assassination.

    "When you body shame me, it really hurts my feelings."

    "Well, I'm just a horrible mother; I bet you are just waiting for me to die!"

- Giving the other person ulterior motives.

    "I think you should go home; you have had way too much to drink."

    "You are just jealous I'm about to get laid, and no girl has even talked to you all night!"

- What-about-isms.

  "What about the food I buy, isn't that enough? You are so ungrateful!"

- Threats when someone doesn't do what you want or expect.

  "If you break up with me, I'm going to kill myself! I'll make you sorry!"

Whether it's an insult or a full-blown threat, you have placed people in impossible and stressful situations because of your emotional dysregulation. Let's practice a bit of empathy. Imagine how you would feel at your job if someone put words in your mouth or trivially threatened your livelihood. Say you wanted to take a trip with your well-earned vacation days. You planned it and filled out the proper paperwork. Then thanks to the incompetence of upper management, there is more work than anticipated on the days you are set to be out. You explain the situation and are, for all intents and purposes, totally in the right for taking your days as planned. Instead of telling management to sit and spin, you calmly and professionally lay out the facts and know for a fact that not only is this not your fault or responsibility, but anyone else can handle the fire while you are away. Instead of management wishing you safe travels, you are met with:

- *"Ugh, I have to do everything around here."*

- *"Well, I guess we can all drown while you sip a cocktail on the beach."*

- *"We are a family; how can you do this to us?"*

- *"What about all the sacrifices I have made for you?"*

- *"I guess you don't care about your career."*

You are probably getting annoyed just reading this; imagine being put on the spot like that in real life.

Wanting To Be Right Outweighs Being Happy

At their core, a vulnerable narcissist knows that they feel inadequate. They do their damndest to cover it up, but it always ends up peeking through. Having faith in other people is inconceivable because it creates the risk of being duped. It's humiliating to be proven wrong by someone you trust. Instead, they decide it's easier to just prove themselves right. They push people away on purpose because if ending up alone is guaranteed, then it is preferable to have some control over that fact. It's a classic self-fulfilling prophecy. This fear manifests in insults, irritation, and resentment. In the end, a narcissist ends up alone, but at least they can hang their hat on knowing all along that this relationship would never last.

Unwittingly Exposing Yourself

It only takes a split second, but when you lose your footing, you instantly lose face. In a high pressure situation, you cannot be the first to blink. A stammer, a mistake, or flawed logic is catnip for your opponent. That opening is something they can latch onto, and a narcissist with no ability to regulate their emotions will take the bait. Your arguments become weaker and will eventually devolve into personal attacks and logical fallacies and there are only two ways this can end. You capitulate (this is the best case scenario) or you freak out and dig yourself into a deeper hole because you cannot stop winding yourself up.

Narcissistic Collapse

The final step of a narcissist's emotional dysregulation is an acute state of distress called "narcissistic collapse". This is the moment where the narcissist is cornered, and their worst fear is realized–they are exposed to everyone. The narcissist may experience overwhelming shame, humiliation, and emptiness during a collapse as their carefully curated self-image crumbles. They may exhibit depressive symptoms, socially withdraw, and lose interest in previously valued activities. This collapse can catalyze self-reflection and the possibility of personal growth, but it can also lead to increased vulnerability, volatile behaviors, and attempts to regain a sense of superiority. This is not a run-of-the-mill social faux pas. It will require an immense amount of work to recover. You will need a support network; you cannot push them away for your own sake (Nicole Arzt, 2023).

Sometimes Progress Seems Futile

Michael: Why can't you accept that she might be living a good, honest life?

Eleanor Shellstrop: Because I wanted that mom... If Donna Shellstrop has truly changed, then that means she was always capable of change, but I just wasn't worth changing for.

—The Good Place

One of the most unpleasant realities of changing as a person is that not everyone may accept these changes. To you, a conscious effort to be better is hard work. You are free of your demons and are finally seeing things. Your self-esteem may improve due to having a more balanced way of thinking and legitimate pride in your progress. Unfortunately, others, especially those affected by your behavior, may not see it that way. To them, this is how you should have been this whole time. If anything, your development may rub salt in the wounds as you proved that you could always be this person but chose not to. This is not an entirely fair assessment, but this is where empathy comes into play.

This rejection of genuine effort can send anyone into a tailspin, let alone someone who deals with narcissism. Still, you must choose to respect that point of view. We usually don't congratulate someone for going an entire day without harming someone. At this point, you should give this person space and continue to look inward for motivation. What you cannot do is undo your progress because people aren't responding in the way you thought. You may not see it, but you may ask for profound forgiveness even though you have changed. Some people may not be ready or never will be, and that it is their prerogative. You have to be willing to give that person the same grace that you expect from them. If not, you may close that door forever and prove you have learned nothing.

Group Therapy

It's easy for narcissists to think that no one understands their struggles. Luckily, group therapy can change all that. It may seem like a bad idea to gather a group of narcissists in one room and have them hash out their problems. However, with a skilled therapist at the helm, it will look more like a round table of gentlemen than a game of *Survivor*. In these groups, a narcissist can see what progress can look like as they commiserate over their shared experiences and struggles. This is excellent practice in learning to lean on someone else and becoming vulnerable in front of a group. In this setting, they will receive feedback and offer their advice with a provider looking on to ensure that everyone in the group remains on even footing and that the advice being doled out is good. This is an excellent opportunity for self-reflection, as a narcissist can see their struggles in another person, which makes them both more tangible and easier to digest (Julia Childs Heyl, 2022).

Key Takeaways

- Narcissists often experience emotional dysregulation, leading to destructive behavior for themselves and others.

- Understanding the root causes of anger in narcissism, such as shame, weakness, and fear of rejection, can help manage these emotions.

- Narcissists would rather be right over happy and will push people away to maintain control.

- Unwittingly exposing vulnerabilities can lead to a narcissist's emotional collapse.

- Progress may be met with resistance from others, but you must stay committed to self-improvement and respect others' perspectives.

- Group therapy can be beneficial for narcissists to gain insight and support from like-minded people.

HUNGER FOR VALIDATION MAKES YOU A GLUTTON FOR PUNISHMENT

"When the healthy pursuit of self-interest and self-realization turns into self-absorption, other people can lose their intrinsic value in our eyes and become mere means to the fulfillment of our needs and desires."

- P.M. FORNI

Narcissism has an insidious way of stealing your identity. This disorder does not survive in a vacuum, it feeds on validation. It can be in the form of adoration, attention, or pity. The only rule is that the narcissist must be seen in a good light. As a result, your identity can become a fickle thing. You aren't doing things because you are passionate or to be true to yourself. You do them because it feeds that hunger for attention. Despite how far you get in life, you might still feel empty. It's because you have never lived for yourself, and the back of your brain knows it.

Living as a Chameleon

Because you try to appeal to everyone, you shift your personality depending on who you are with and what will give you the most social capital. In school, did you ever have (or were you) a friend who was great individually but became a nightmare when they were around another, more assertive personality? They would gang up on you, making your head spin. On the one hand, you have one person who is predictable in their mistreatment of you. On the other hand, the two-faced friend was just at your house, doing homework and confiding in each other.

The two-faced friend values you as a source of validation but with stark differences. This person sees a form of friendship and companionship with a gentler, more stable, and easy person. As a result, they feed off that ease and know they can take advantage of the gentle friend's trust, loyalty, and insecurities by having less-than-ideal friends. Meanwhile, they see the stronger friend as a form of social currency and upward movement. They know they must play a game to stay in their good graces. If they don't, then they will start being victimized as well.

So, what is the true identity of the two-faced friend? Are they a hurt person seeking comfort in another person, or are they a backstabber who would climb over their mother for a bit of clout? It's hard to say; most likely, the two-faced friend would say the former as an adult because it is a convenient way to justify hurting a person who cared about them. This pattern is not just prevalent in narcissists, but it is a straightforward way to illustrate the effect of the disorder. Imagine this, but with every person in your life. Every interaction is a game. You must pick who to latch on to, who is worth placating, who can be discarded, and who can tolerate your behavior. Unlike most people, you are willing to be a one-person band in the story of your life. Worst of all, you are not only playing with different aspects of your personality, you have probably lied and exaggerated the whole way there, and now you must keep all that straight.

Selective Memory

Let's examine the techniques narcissists use to get people on their side. The first is not a lie, but it's taking a microscope to the whole truth and only observing whatever suits them. Let's say you are in an argument about getting a new car. Your partner lays out the reasons why it's a bad idea. It's not in the budget, the old car is fine, it will be a pain to maintain, it's not practical, etc. You have been arguing for an hour and your partner is exhausted. They finally say, "You know what, I don't care", and walk away. Now most people would know that this does not translate into a blessing to go get the car. But a narcissist might now go out and buy the gas guzzler because they have heard the thing they wanted and can now reflect it back. The narcissist may not even be aware they are doing this and will be shocked when their partner flips out at having another depreciating asset in their possession.

Depending on the type of narcissism, this can manifest in different ways. More grandiose narcissists will tend to remember positive things and throw out the negative. Meanwhile, covert narcissists will remember and fixate on every slight they have ever experienced from legitimate grudges to a cashier that looked at them funny (Krusemark et al., 2015). This can be massively frustrating to the people around them who know what they said but are now being gaslighted into thinking that they weren't clear enough or are to blame for the miscommunication. The reality is that a narcissist will twist reality enough to hear what they want to hear to get that validation. This sort of behavior will destroy relationships in time because the typical person will not be able to deal with the instability and anxiety that comes with having to live in two states of reality. Remember, being a narcissist does not mean you are not capable of love, and it will hurt when the person rightfully collects their things and leaves.

Doing the Bare Minimum

Being in a healthy relationship is work and narcissists know this. You might have found yourself testing people's tolerance for how much of yourself you need to give to keep them around. Not only that, you might want a parade and thanks for doing things that are expected of others, which other people may not be inclined to give. This bare minimum can change from person to person which can become confusing for everyone involved.

This is classically seen in mixed families where step parenting is involved. To a narcissist, their biological child is an extension of themselves so they will naturally treat them better. The biological child will get all the attention and have all of their flaws erased. Meanwhile, the stepchild becomes the scapegoat. A narcissist may not see this person as important, just a person they are forced to live with. They allow them very little leeway, always blame them for everything and magnify their flaws. The child cannot leave, so their tolerance to this behavior does not matter. What does matter is what their partner thinks.

Depending on how involved the partner is with their child's life, they may not see the extent of the behavior and when the child starts acting out, they can then be painted as the problem by the parent. Meanwhile the stepparent wants the praise and adoration for raising the stepchild. They are the ones that were generous enough to marry someone with their own children, commit to raising them, and take the financial burdens that come with raising a whole human. In reality though, the child never asked for any of this. The adults made a choice, but the child, with no power or influence, is often the one to pay for it. So, which is the real identity, the doting parent and loving partner, or a monster in the master bedroom? Why would some take on this responsibility if they don't love everything that comes with their partner?

Truthfully, it's the idea of being in a relationship that they love as well as the identity of being a graceful parent that swoops in and gives a child a two parent home. It's all about societal approval, no matter the cost. If they didn't care about what people thought, then they would never agree to such a radical life change and take on a role they know they cannot fulfill. So, they make it as easy as possible on themselves while letting everyone know how challenging their life is.

Performing and Weaponizing Being a Good Person

Narcissists with a bit more self-awareness know that society tends to find good people more palatable. Since empathy can be out of reach, narcissists will perform what they think people want to see while adding a spice of grandiosity. While we have established that practicing empathy is essential for a narcissist to heal, this is not the same thing. One is an effort to learn a behavior in an effort to adapt it and become a better person. The other is weaponizing goodwill. In the end, it's about what you hope to get out of the interaction and if the answer is maintaining an image or manipulating someone, then you know where you stand.

A very modern phenomenon is the weaponization of "therapy speak" to justify bad behavior. In recent years, therapy has become normalized, which is great. People are learning the language of their mind and are getting better at communicating their emotions and putting up boundaries. This is great for a therapist's office or difficult conversations where you need to succinctly explain your thought process when you previously had difficulty doing so. However, it can be bastardized by people who want to take this language of understanding and turn it into a language of justification (Tayo Bero, 2023).

While the rise in mental health awareness has been a blessing, some took it as an opportunity to add a new vocabulary to manipulate. Ordinarily, when people aren't in sync with their loved ones, they may push back on an idea slightly or just roll with the punches because they care about the person. At worst, a mild disagreement can happen, but it's typically resolved. The narcissist takes it to the nth degree and accuses the person of abusive behavior, not because they genuinely feel like a victim, but because they know that flowery therapy speak is tricky to dispute. It puts the other person on the defensive because no one likes being labeled an abuser. The offending incident can be relatively minor, but that hasn't stopped narcissists from creating a volcano out of a molehill.

- *You promised to wash the dishes since I had to work a double.*

    ○ *You are just like my mom, constantly criticizing me! It's triggering!*

- *Hey, I'm really hurt you did not show up to my birthday party.*

- ○ *Look, I was putting down a boundary. I didn't have the emotional bandwidth to cancel. Why can't you respect that?!*

- *I gave you plenty of lead time and offered you an extension. If you couldn't complete the assignment, you should have asked for help.*

- ○ *You know I have ADHD and part of that is time management issues; it's not my fault I was set up to fail.*

Something that narcissists need to come to terms with is that two things can be true at once. They can have some internal struggles and get their feelings hurt, but they refuse to digest the criticism and see it from the other person's perspective. Other people are allowed to feel hurt, abandoned, and mistreated by your behavior, regardless of the source.

You can have the world's saddest backstory with bones made of glass and a wicked stepmother who made you clean litter boxes in a full body cast, but that is never an excuse to hurt other people. New people are a blessing and a unique chance to engage in the human experience of community, but you will never do that if you continue to project and blame your long-standing issues on someone you just met. Yes, critiques hurt, and everyone gets defensive, but that swell of emotions tends to quell a bit when you realize that they have a point, and you now have actionable feedback.

These therapy topics are valid and should be discussed with the people in your life if you are comfortable, but if you find yourself using them to win an argument, you have lost the plot of therapy. It can be liberating to find the words for the experiences you have been having, and it's tempting to fully assimilate these words into your identity. This is another way you are letting your past and disorder consume you. You will never make progress if you use these revelations as a shield instead of a sword. These are tools for healing, not weapons. Use them accordingly.

But I'm an Empath!

One distinct flavor of the above phenomenon is the insistence that you are inherently special due to some God-given ability. Maybe you are a natural genius, creative. The empath is a modern example of this, thanks to the rise of therapy speak and the romanticization of mental health. This is more than just empathy, which is a skill that can be honed. People claim they can sense another person's emotions as if it's happening to them. Instead of just being good at reading people (which is impressive enough on its own), a narcissist will go through the extra effort to frame it as this gift they can use to heal others.

This is classic overcompensation that more and more people are becoming wise to. You don't have to try and be something if you are inherently unique. Your empathy makes you great, and your intelligence makes you trustworthy. These are also claims you don't need to prove, especially if you aim to attract someone more vulnerable than you. You effectively put yourself on a pedestal and enjoy the reverence. This tact stops working though the second you face any resistance. An emotionally intelligent person recognizes that an empath (which is rare and even debatable in its existence) would not need to announce they are an empath. They realize that their friend in need doesn't need their super-powered buddy to feel around their brain and deliver custom wisdom, they need a shoulder to cry on and an ear to listen to them.

Lessons From Monsters 4
The Stauffer Parents

Family vloggers exist to give parents an image of an ideal life. The parents always look perfect, with their weirdly white homes, flawless parenting, and palatable content that can be monetized to sell ads. There has been a lot of discourse around the subject as people are just coming around to the fact that shoving a camera in a child's face at every milestone, tantrum, embarrassing moment, and punishment is put online for the entire planet to consume. However, no other channel has shown the sinister side of narcissistic parents hunting for validation in the form of ad revenue and clicks than the Stauffer family.

The Stauffer family were successful family vloggers with hundreds of thousands of subscribers and sponsorships. Their vlogs were focused on their children, documenting their every move, home-schooling, and vegan meals. Thumbnails were splashed with multiple iterations of their best-surprised face every time their children did something mildly interesting. Titles such as COFFEE PROBLEMS | COFFEE PROBLEMS, RELATIVES ARE THE WORST graced their pages and were eaten up by viewers. Still, they felt something was missing from their clan and decided they could expand their family and get some heartwarming content in the process.

They couldn't just adopt any child; they needed to go full martyr. They chose a child with special needs and, for months, dedicated vlogs to the adoption process and preparing a home for this poor child. They were scooping them up from a hopeless situation and shepherding them into the American dream. People tried to dissuade her from adopting him, calling his case severe, but Mika was a former nurse. She specifically chose from a group of kids listed as severe cases and insisted she could handle it. The family even went on to fundraise to pay for the adoption costs (despite their already high income). Huxley Stauffer became a family member after some time and a lot of ad revenue. They celebrated his "Gotcha Day" (a term hated by the adoption community because it typically refers to pets) but were unaware of the storm that awaited them.

From what the Stauffers claimed, the agency stated that Huxley's disability was born from a brain tumor that profoundly affected his development. When discussing their struggles adapting to him, it seemed like they expected a child with challenges who was ultimately docile. Instead, Huxley never had a tumor at all; he was severely autistic.

Any parent would jump for joy, especially since Mika said she could handle a challenging diagnosis. Huxley would face his hardships, but he wasn't terminal. Except this threw a wrench in their whole savior plan. Huxley did not fit into the Stauffer's image of a perfect family. He would have meltdowns and be traumatized by food insecurity. Thus, he could not be vlogged in a way that would be palatable for the audience. Huxley would start appearing in fewer videos, and soon something amazing happened; the Stauffers became pregnant again. So, what were they to do now that one child had no purpose, and they had a new fresh baby on the way?

Audiences noticed the seams coming undone when the family vacationed in Bali without Huxley. It was a questionable decision since they gained many new subscribers from the adoption process. They were left to scratch their heads until a thumbnail showed both Stauffer parents in tears wearing white t-shirts, surrounded by a bedroom resembling a white void. They went on to explain that Huxley's case was more than they had bargained for, but not to worry because Huxley was in his new "forever home." Yes, they rehomed a child they traveled across the globe to adopt like a dog they didn't want anymore. They did their best to justify their decision saying that Huxley's meltdowns were challenging and traumatizing for the children. No one denies that Huxley was a complex case; no parent asks for this. Except in their hubris, the Stauffers did explicitly ask for this. They never considered their lifestyle, other children, or the adoptee. Some of the discourse says that the parents were banking on Huxley passing from complications from his brain tumor, giving them more sympathy and martyr points.

They dehumanized this child and saw him as little more than a pet they could train to be on camera and garner their views. Ultimately, this scandal made national news, destroying their channel and reputation. The channel is defunct, and the Stauffers' image as the perfect parents are forever shattered (The Right Opinion, 2020).

What Dictates Ethical Actions

Moral philosophers have argued about what makes an action ethical for thousands of years. The act of charity can be severely skewed based on who your favorite philosopher is.

- **Consequentialism:** This school of thought measures the ethics of an action based on the intrinsic (utility) value of the action instead of the motivation. Think of a charitable act as a three-part structure. There is the motivator, the charity itself, and the implications.

- **Deontology:** This argues that ethics are nothing more than a social contract, and we should engage in it because we participate in a society that relies on it to function. A tithe at a stricter church can be an example of this. People don't necessarily donate because they want to; they are bound to the rules of their church to do so. Assuming the money goes to the poor and not the pastor's jet, is the act any less moral?

- **Virtue ethics:** An act is judged based on the motive or character of the act rather than its direct consequences.

Let's say we come across someone collecting money to build wheelchairs for dogs. Consequentialism argues that even if you post yourself on social media putting a dollar in the box, the act is still ethical because, ultimately, a dog gets its wheelchair (Sinnott-Armstrong, 2022). Virtue ethics would criticize the action even though the result is the same because you might not have given anything if you did not get to display your act on social media. Deontology argues that a person should always set aside cash for dogs in wheelchairs because a society where a dog could not get around after a catastrophic injury would not be just.

Consequentialism and deontology are good starter ethics for someone who needs to practice determining an ethical act. Their simplicity, though, has made them targets of criticism. Critics argue that they depersonalize the act and ironically can result in asking too much of the giving person (Alexander & Moore, 2021). For example, a person might not have the money to give because they gave it to someone else, or maybe they didn't want to donate that money for dogs in wheelchairs that month (which is everyone's prerogative). It also assumes that the consequences will always be good. For example, maybe one of the dogs you gave a wheelchair to might seek to destroy humanity and could only do so because it gained mobility–was your charity unethical based on the negative consequences?

This is why narcissists should try to graduate to virtue ethics or do good things because they are good people, not just because they feel obligated to society or to gain karmic brownie points. You need to be guided by consciousness, which requires believing in your moral compass, especially if charity and compassion are new concepts (Hursthouse & Pettigrove, 2022).

Stealth Charity

The antidote to gluttony is charity, but this act can be corrupted if you are not careful. Everyone should do their best to pay it forward and give what they are comfortable with, whether time or money. For a recovering narcissist, giving can help you think beyond only helping yourself. This should not be a passive process where you set a recurring payment of a dollar to autopay and call it a day.

It would help if you connected to the thing your charity benefits, whether it's visiting the website and going through the mission statements and testimonials or going over and volunteering time. Coming face to face with the people (or animals) you are helping will help your brain connect the dots that your act of charity can have an effect more significant than just feeling good. Whether it's the smile on someone's face at a soup kitchen or a litter of kittens that will now have housing and food, it all matters in the end, which can be a struggle for a narcissist to see. Be careful, though, not to warp these feelings into further narcissism.

No one likes performative activism, even if there is a net positive to it. We have all cringed at influencers posting themselves giving a dollar to an unhoused person. People will always be suspicious of people who care for the less fortunate, especially if the charitable act does not match the volume, you are projecting these acts. It can come off as compensatory. No one who is satisfied with how much they have given will need external validation. Charity and volunteering are not only good for society, but they also stimulate your brain to release endorphins. People like helping others; that is a biological fact, and the act alone should be enough (*Why Giving Is Good For Your Health*, 2022).

Narcissists who have trouble with self-actualization may seek that validation from others, tainting the act even though everyone feels good after voluntarily giving something of themselves. People may need to realize that you need that external source and chalk up your projecting of good deeds as a form of attention-grabbing. You have to resist this urge and keep charitable acts private, especially if you want to work out your self-validation muscle. This means not posting receipts of charitable donations, posting pictures of yourself on your social media at a soup kitchen, or maneuvering the conversation around how grateful you are compared to those you help. It's okay to talk about the organization or the act but keep it objective. Avoid making the service about you; talk about it with the people you are helping in the spotlight.

Key Takeaways

- Narcissism thrives on validation, even if it's at the cost of personal identity.

- Narcissists engage in selective memory, focusing on aspects that validate their desired worldview and chucking away negative information.

- Narcissists often do the bare minimum in relationships and expect praise for expected behaviors, leading to confusion and resentment.

- Narcissists may start to weaponize the moral high ground, using therapy language and claiming special abilities for the sake of manipulation.

- Ethical actions should be guided by virtue ethics, where one acts out of genuine goodwill, rather than obligation or moral dessert.

- Charity and service can be a way for narcissists to break free from their self-centered mindset. The caveat is being careful to not trade one form of narcissism for another.

- Keeping charitable acts private and focusing on the impact rather than personal recognition is important to maintain the integrity of the act and avoid further narcissistic tendencies.

CONCLUSION

Exploring the nature of your narcissism can provide profound insights into your destructive patterns and their impact on your life. Even if your narcissism was born from an unhappy start, you can still work towards a better future. The journey towards healing involves embracing self-reflection, vulnerability, cultivating a support network, and, most importantly, actually believing in yourself and not the image you have created. Therapy and studying ethics can give you the tools to break free of a narcissistic mindset. You have to learn to think about everyone, including yourself, with kindness. Only then can you foster real self-esteem and forge long-lasting relationships.

While You're Here

May I ask you the **small favor** to leave a quick **review or rating** on Amazon?

Even though the simple act of leaving a review will take you **less than a minute**, it will give a huge amount of support, and as an independent author **I appreciate the of your time and your empathy more than you know**!

To make it quick and easy, when you scan one of the QR codes below it will take you directly to your Amazon review page.

Amazon Review US **Amazon Review UK**

Thank you for your help and support.

Best Wishes,

- Lucas

Remember that you can download your 2 free gifts by scanning the QR code at the beginning of the book.

REFERENCES

Alexander, L., & Moore, M. (2021). Deontological

    Ethics. In E. N. Zalta (Ed.), *The Stanford*

    Encyclopedia of Philosophy (Winter 2021).

    Metaphysics Research Lab, Stanford University.

    https://plato.stanford.edu/archives/win2021/e

    ntries/ethics-deontological/

Bamelis, L. L. M., Evers, S. M. A. A., Spinhoven, P., &

    Arntz, A. (2014). Results of a multicenter

    randomized controlled trial of the clinical

    effectiveness of schema therapy for personality

    disorders. *The American Journal of Psychiatry*,

171(3), 305–322.

https://doi.org/10.1176/appi.ajp.2013.1204051
8

Ben Westhoff. (2017). *Original Gangstas.* Hachette
Books.

Body Language – Narcissism and how to survive it.
(2018, March 13).

http://narcissistory.com/?p=437

Britta Zeltmann. (2023, January 7). *Eerie similarities
between Idaho suspect and Brian Laundrie
revealed by expert.* The US Sun.
https://www.the-
sun.com/news/7072430/idaho-suspect-bryan-
kohberger-brian-laundrie-body-language/

Cascio, C. N., Konrath, S. H., & Falk, E. B. (2015).
Narcissists' social pain seen only in the brain.
Social Cognitive and Affective Neuroscience,
10(3), 335–341.

https://doi.org/10.1093/scan/nsu072

Chester, D. S., & DeWall, C. N. (2016). Sound the
Alarm: The Effect of Narcissism on Retaliatory
Aggression Is Moderated by dACC Reactivity to
Rejection. *Journal of Personality*, *84*(3), 361–
368. https://doi.org/10.1111/jopy.12164

Coleman, D., Lawrence, R., Parekh, A., Galfalvy, H.,
Blasco-Fontecilla, H., Brent, D. A., Mann, J. J.,
Baca-Garcia, E., & Oquendo, M. A. (2017).
Narcissistic Personality Disorder and Suicidal
Behavior in Mood Disorders. *Journal of
Psychiatric Research*, *85*, 24–28.
https://doi.org/10.1016/j.jpsychires.2016.10.02
0

Dieckmann, E., & Behary, W. (2015). Schematherapie:
Ein Ansatz zur Behandlung narzisstischer
Persönlichkeitsstörungen. *Fortschritte der
Neurologie · Psychiatrie*, *83*(08), 463–478.

https://doi.org/10.1055/s-0035-1553484

Dr. Todd Grande (Director). (2018, June 19). *Cognitive Behavioral Strategies for Narcissistic Personality Disorder*. https://www.youtube.com/watch?v=JRcBHcFK XmE

Edelstein, R. S., Yim, I. S., & Quas, J. A. (2010). Narcissism Predicts Heightened Cortisol Reactivity to a Psychosocial Stressor in Men. *Journal of Research in Personality*, *44*(5), 565– 572. https://doi.org/10.1016/j.jrp.2010.06.008

Ekua Hagan. (2018). *What Do Narcissists See When They Look in the Mirror? | Psychology Today*. https://www.psychologytoday.com/us/blog/the -clarity/201809/what-do-narcissists-see-when-they-look-in-the-mirror

Emmons, R. A., & Stern, R. (2013). Gratitude as a Psychotherapeutic Intervention: Gratitude.

Journal of Clinical Psychology, 69(8), 846–855. https://doi.org/10.1002/jclp.22020

Greg Kading. (2011). *Murder Rap: The Untold Story of the Biggie Smalls & Tupac Shakur Murder Investigations by the Detective Who Solved Both Cases.* One Time Publishing.

Harlow, H. F., Dodsworth, R. O., & Harlow, M. K. (1965). Total social isolation in monkeys. *Proceedings of the National Academy of Sciences, 54*(1), 90–97. https://doi.org/10.1073/pnas.54.1.90

Heidi Butler. (2022). *Golden Child vs Scapegoat: When Parents Pick Favorites - FamilyEducation.* https://www.familyeducation.com/family-life/relationships/siblings/the-golden-child-vs-the-scapegoat-when-parents-pick-favorites

Hörz-Sagstetter, S., Diamond, D., Clarkin, J. F., Levy, K. N., Rentrop, M., Fischer-Kern, M., Cain, N. M.,

& Doering, S. (2018). Clinical Characteristics of Comorbid Narcissistic Personality Disorder in Patients With Borderline Personality Disorder. *Journal of Personality Disorders*, *32*(4), 562–575. https://doi.org/10.1521/pedi_2017_31_306

Hursthouse, R., & Pettigrove, G. (2022). Virtue Ethics. In E. N. Zalta & U. Nodelman (Eds.), *The Stanford Encyclopedia of Philosophy* (Winter 2022). Metaphysics Research Lab, Stanford University. https://plato.stanford.edu/archives/win2022/entries/ethics-virtue/

Jack Jones. (2000). *Let Me Take You Down: Inside the Mind of Mark David Chapman, the Man Who Killed John Lennon* (1st ed.). Random House Publishing Group.

Jauk, E., & Dieterich, R. (2019). Addiction and the Dark

Triad of Personality. *Frontiers in Psychiatry*, *10*. https://www.frontiersin.org/articles/10.3389/f psyt.2019.00662

Jill Krasny. (2014, May 30). *Why You Don't Need Rich Customers to Sell Luxury Goods*. Inc.Com. https://www.inc.com/jill-krasny/the-trap-of-luxury.html

Joe Sharkey. (2018). *Death Sentence: The Inside Story of the John List Murders*. Open Road Media.

John Carreyrou. (2020). *Bad Blood: Secrets and Lies in a Silicon Valley Startup*. Knopf Doubleday Publishing Group.

Johnson, R., & Cureton, A. (2022). Kant's Moral Philosophy. In E. N. Zalta & U. Nodelman (Eds.), *The Stanford Encyclopedia of Philosophy* (Fall 2022). Metaphysics Research Lab, Stanford University.

https://plato.stanford.edu/archives/fall2022/e
ntries/kant-moral/

Julia Childs Heyl. (2022). *Finding a Narcissistic Abuse
Support Group*. Verywell Mind.
https://www.verywellmind.com/how-to-find-a-
narcissistic-abuse-support-group-5271477

Karyl McBride. (2011). *The Narcissistic Family Tree |
Psychology Today*.
https://www.psychologytoday.com/us/blog/the
-legacy-distorted-love/201105/the-narcissistic-
family-tree

Kelsey, R. M., Ornduff, S. R., McCann, C. M., & Reiff, S.
(2001). Psychophysiological characteristics of
narcissism during active and passive coping.
Psychophysiology, 38(2), 292–303.

Kristin Neff. (2011). *Why Self-Compassion May Be the
Antidote to Narcissism | Psychology Today*.
https://www.psychologytoday.com/us/blog/the

-power-self-compassion/201106/why-self-

compassion-may-be-the-antidote-narcissism

Krusemark, E. A., Lee, C., & Newman, J. P. (2015).

Narcissism dimensions differentially moderate

selective attention to evaluative stimuli in

incarcerated offenders. *Personality Disorders*,

6(1), 12–21.

https://doi.org/10.1037/per0000087

Luo, Y. L. L., Cai, H., & Song, H. (2014). A Behavioral

Genetic Study of Intrapersonal and

Interpersonal Dimensions of Narcissism. *PLOS*

ONE, *9*(4), e93403.

https://doi.org/10.1371/journal.pone.0093403

Mayo Clinic. (n.d.). *Narcissistic personality disorder—*

Symptoms and causes. Mayo Clinic. Retrieved

June 12, 2023, from

https://www.mayoclinic.org/diseases-

conditions/narcissistic-personality-disorder/symptoms-causes/syc-20366662

McLean, J. (2007). Psychotherapy with a Narcissistic Patient Using Kohut's Self Psychology Model. *Psychiatry (Edgmont)*, 4(10), 40–47.

Mück, M., Mattes, A., Porth, E., & Stahl, J. (2023). Narcissism and the perception of failure – evidence from the error-related negativity and the error positivity. *Personality Neuroscience*, 6, e2. https://doi.org/10.1017/pen.2022.7

Nicole Arzt. (2023). *What Is Narcissistic Collapse?* Choosing Therapy. https://www.choosingtherapy.com/narcissistic-collapse/

Poonam Sachdev. (2021). *What Is Transference?* WebMD. https://www.webmd.com/mental-health/what-is-transference

Robert Rand. (2018). *The Menendez Murders: The Shocking Untold Story of the Menendez Family and the Killings that Stunned the Nation.* Penguin Random House.

Ronningstam, E., & Baskin-Sommers, A. R. (2013). Fear and decision-making in narcissistic personality disorder—A link between psychoanalysis and neuroscience. *Dialogues in Clinical Neuroscience, 15*(2), 191–201.

Sedikides, C., & Hart, C. M. (2022). Narcissism and conspicuous consumption. *Current Opinion in Psychology, 46*, 101322. https://doi.org/10.1016/j.copsyc.2022.101322

Sinnott-Armstrong, W. (2022). Consequentialism. In E. N. Zalta & U. Nodelman (Eds.), *The Stanford Encyclopedia of Philosophy* (Winter 2022). Metaphysics Research Lab, Stanford University. https://plato.stanford.edu/archives/win2022/entries/consequentialism/

Sivanathan, D., Bizumic, B., Rieger, E., & Huxley, E.

(2019). Vulnerable narcissism as a mediator of the relationship between perceived parental invalidation and eating disorder pathology. *Eating and Weight Disorders - Studies on Anorexia, Bulimia and Obesity, 24*(6), 1071–1077. https://doi.org/10.1007/s40519-019-00647-2

Smokey Glow (Director). (2021, December 9). *INTERNET HISTORY: Dramagedon 2 (Part 2).* https://www.youtube.com/watch?v=8voGBxSG iYM

Sommer, K. L., Kirkland, K. L., Newman, S. R., Estrella, P., & Andreassi, J. L. (2009). Narcissism and Cardiovascular Reactivity to Rejection Imagery1. *Journal of Applied Social Psychology, 39*(5), 1083–1115. https://doi.org/10.1111/j.1559-1816.2009.00473.x

Tayo Bero. (2023, February 2). The Problem with Therapy Speak. *Chatelaine.* https://chatelaine.com/living/therapy-speak/

The Neuroscience of Narcissism and Narcissistic Abuse | CPTSDfoundation.org. (2020, June 15). https://cptsdfoundation.org/2020/06/22/the-neuroscience-of-narcissism-and-narcissistic-abuse/

The Right Opinion (Director). (2020, November 5). *The Family YouTuber Who Gave Away Her Son— Myka Stauffer | TRO.* https://www.youtube.com/watch?v=8dTRx9Ys bwA

Torgersen, S., Myers, J., Reichborn-Kjennerud, T., Røysamb, E., Kubarych, T. S., & Kendler, K. S. (2012). The Heritability of Cluster B Personality Disorders Assessed Both by Personal Interview and Questionnaire. *Journal of Personality*

Disorders, *26*(6), 848–866.

https://doi.org/10.1521/pedi.2012.26.6.848

Why Giving Is Good For Your Health. (2022, December 7). Cleveland Clinic. https://health.clevelandclinic.org/why-giving-is-good-for-your-health/

Zalman, H., Doorn, K. A., & Eubanks, C. F. (2019). Alliance challenges in the treatment of a narcissistic patient: The case of Alex. *Research in Psychotherapy : Psychopathology, Process, and Outcome*, *22*(2), 351. https://doi.org/10.4081/ripppo.2019.351

Zauraiz Lone. (2019, September 20). *Freud and the Nature of Narcissism*. Psych Central. https://psychcentral.com/pro/freud-and-the-nature-of-narcissism

Made in United States
Troutdale, OR
11/01/2024

24323884R00108